SYKESVILLE

PAST & PRESENT

A Walking Tour

By Linda F. Greenberg

Copyright © 2000
Brinkmann Publishing LLC
605 Gaither Road
Sykesville, MD 21784
(410) 442-1537

Second Edition

Manufactured in the United States of America.

ISBN 0-9678905-0-0

TABLE OF CONTENTS

MAPS

Sykesville

By its side Patapsco flows,
And up its hills the shadows
run.
Every garden bears a rose,
And lovely is the Carroll sun:
Here the B. & O. goes by,
Here the little valleys sing;
And Sykesville is a town of sky,
Of busy people on the wing.

An elevator filled with grain,
Apple butter, feed and grist;
River rising in the rain,
Little veils of sun and mist:
Granite churches set above
On their hilltops of the day,

Teaching truth and trust and love
Every week and every way.

Smiling neighbors on the street,
Friendly people everywhere;
Trying to make their life complete,
Trying to struggle through their care:
Like a jewel within a bowl,
O'er her all the little hills
Seem to hover like a soul
Guarding here from all the ills.

--From the "Good Morning" column
by Folger McKinsey, the Bentztown
Bard, of *the Baltimore Sun,* 1941.

iii

Map 1
Sykesville's Location in Carroll County

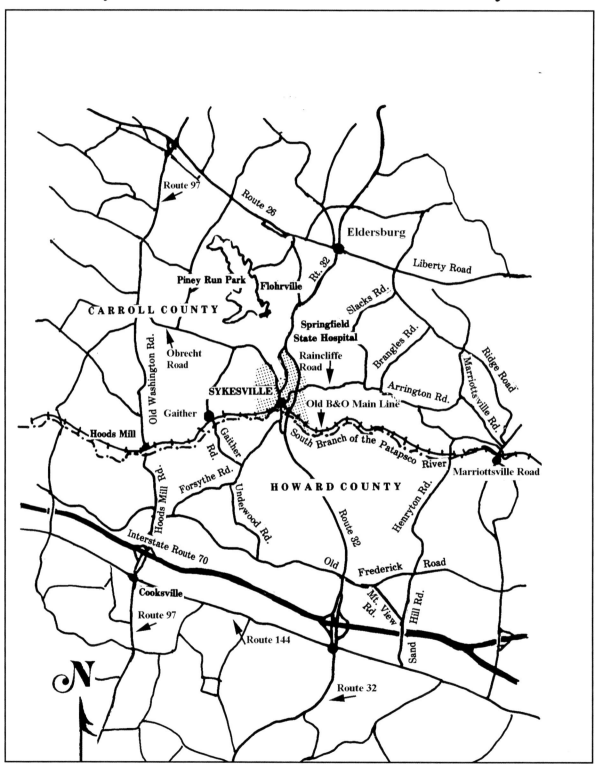

ACKNOWLEDGEMENTS

In *Sykesville: Past & Present* we combine facts about the town, its buildings, and its important events, with the stories of its people. It is the people who lived here in the past and who live here today that we celebrate.

Two people in particular made major contributions to the book: The first is Dorothy Schafer; the second is Harry Sandosky. Mrs. Schafer provided illuminating descriptions of Sykesville's people, and Mr. Sandosky, now deceased, left buildings as testimony to his entrepreneurship.

Dorothy Schafer, a patient and insightful observer, was always gracious and accommodating in sharing information. Mrs. Schafer was born and raised in Sykesville; she attended the town's social events, knew its people, and was aware of their likes and dislikes. When asked about people she knew, or what it was like here in the summertime when she was a teenager, Mrs. Schafer's accounts always balanced the sensibilities of the people she described with the need for accurate reporting. She skillfully wove together facts, people, and values to create a complex and wonderfully textured fabric.

Duane Doxzen contributed the comprehensive Introduction. Duane is a historian with a keen appreciation of Sykesville and what preservation can accomplish.

The growth and decline of towns and cities frequently follow a cyclical pattern. Sykesville grew quickly in the early part of the 20th century and held its own through the late forties. But the town was not prepared for the changes ushered in by America's growing preference for car and truck transportation in the 1950s. Sykesville's decline was noticeable after the building of the Route 32 bypass in 1968. The new road sped cars and trucks past the heart of Sykesville, its Main Street businesses. At the same time, Springfield Hospital reduced its patient population, and in 1972 Hurricane Agnes temporarily destroyed the bridge connecting Main Street with Route 32. Then, in 1975, the Carrolltown Shopping Center opened. All of these events directed attention away from the downtown area.

Harry Sandosky reenergized Sykesville and helped establish new business here. From the 1960s through the 1980s, he repaired and improved buildings, initiated renovations, and invested in new mechanical systems, all at a time when many people asked, "why bother?" Harry never gave up and, as a man of great energy, he accomplished a great deal, to which we are all indebted.

He substantially renovated and rebuilt the Greenberg Building, E. W. Beck's Pub, Lloyd Helt's building, Consolidated Stationary, the Sykesville Video Building, Schatz's Building, Hair 'N Place, and Union National Bank. He also added covered walkways, beautified green areas, and generally contributed to the town's appearance.

George Horvath, cartographer, proved a super sleuth in our quest for information on land sales to James Sykes and in identifying the location of Sykes's hotel. George volunteered to review land deeds and other records in Towson, while I reviewed records in Westminster and Annapolis. He spent many hours documenting land transactions from which he drew maps showing James Sykes's past land ownership, the original course of the Patapsco River, and the original route of the B&O Railroad. Our individual research confirmed each other's work, and we then compared George's maps with Sykesville today. As a result we concluded that James Sykes did not purchase land from William Patterson, and Sykes's Hotel was in Carroll—not Howard—County.

Other contributors to this book are: Puzz Brightwell and her sister Alice Hughlett (née Barnes). Puzz provided the dramatic account of the fire of 1937, photographs of Main Street taken in 1943, and a close reading of the manuscript. The photographs were extremely helpful in documenting building changes on Main Street.

Jim Purman, Curator of the Sykesville Gate House Museum, carefully reviewed the manuscript and made many very helpful suggestions. He also located many photographs for the book.

Russell Shipley collaborated in documenting rural life in the first half of the nineteenth century.

Herbert H. Harwood, Jr., railroad historian, assisted with the history of the B&O Railroad and lent the photograph of the Grasshopper No. 7.

Charles and Bonnie Mullins shared their wealth of information about people and buildings. Todd Brown provided data about the town's banks and the Brown family. Calvin Day and Doug Crist provided interesting information about the milling business in rural Maryland and about the Southern States Cooperative.

Katura Springer provided newspaper clippings, stories, and a great deal of general information about life in Sykesville from the 1940s to the present. Barbara Lilly expanded on the role of the Dorseys and the Black Schoolhouse Project; Wiley Purkey provided architectural information as well as details on his home and the McDonald Block; Harry Haight and Alvin Howes described their businesses and building activities; Rose Icenroad assisted with the description of the Sykesville Federal Savings Association; and Howard Reznick described the grocery store and the Home Furniture stores of his father, Herman. Matt Candland, Town Manager, assisted with maps and general information, and Jonathan Herman, Sykesville's Mayor, shared his technical construction expertise, particularly about the Brown Cottages. Dolly Hughes was consulted by numerous people for her recollections of people, buildings, and events. Ted Campbell reviewed part of the manuscript and made several helpful suggestions. Wayne Gadow graciously lent photographs of 7546 Main Street.

Judy Klein, Charlie and Craig Taylor, Sharon Kemm, Norma Ferguson, Joan Davis, and Michael Kasnia clarified facts and added to the information about their homes.

To be remembered with great appreciation is the work of Healan Barrow and Thelma Wimmer in preparing the first edition of *Sykesville: Past & Present,* published in 1986 .

Helpful resources were the staffs at the Historical Society of Carroll County, the Howard County Historical Society, and the Annapolis Hall of Records.

Bruce Greenberg reviewed the manuscript, photographed the buildings on tour, wrote the captions for the photographs, and merged the text and photographs using Photoshop and Quark Express

Jackie Leister of Leister Graphics helped Bruce learn Quark and design the cover and book style. Cindy Gillis of Do You Graphics assisted Bruce in learning Photoshop.

Leslie Greenberg proofread the manuscript, and Jan Smith masterfully edited the text.

My heartfelt thanks to these people for their appreciation of Sykesville and their helpful contributions.

Linda Greenberg

About The Author

Sykesville is a special place for the author, Linda Greenberg. It is the place she has lived longest; it is the place she calls home; and it is the place where she and her husband raised their two children.

The author appreciates history and letting the facts tell the story. She also appreciates tradition and the values people live by. Sykesville, she believes, is a mixing pot of old and new, where traditions and values meet, and usually accommodate. As she would say, in Sykesville, history is being written, and we are privileged to watch it unfold.

Linda has been active in community life, having served on the Historical District Commission in its formative years and having been a member of the Vestry at St. Barnabas Church; she is currently treasurer there. In addition she serves as secretary to the Sykesville Business Association, the Friends of Old Trinity Cemetery, and the American Association for Individual Investors.

She retired last year as president of Greenberg Shows, Inc., in order to have more time to write. She was also vice president of the Greenberg Publishing Company from 1978 through 1993, and while there edited and authored a number of books.

INTRODUCTION
BY DUANE DOXZEN

The Town of **SYKESVILLE** is located in southeastern Carroll County, Maryland, along the south branch of the Patapsco River, just four miles north of the interchange of Interstate 70 and Route 32. Sykesville was incorporated in 1904.

In the early 1800s, the area known as Sykesville consisted of a few buildings—several mills and a few homes adjacent to or near the river. At that time the sparsely settled area was part of Baltimore County. When Carroll County was created in 1837, Sykesville became part of the Freedom District.

James Sykes, considered the town's founding father, was born into a prominent merchant family and came to the area from Baltimore in the late 1820s. He was attracted by the area's economic prospects. Sykesville was located on the new Baltimore & Ohio (B&O) Railroad line that connected Baltimore with points west and served points in between as well. The area offered access to water to run mills and fertile fields for agricultural development. Sykes began purchasing tracts of land, and by 1850 had accumulated considerable landholdings.

The town's commercial center developed slowly on both sides of the Patapsco River. By 1831, Sykes had rebuilt an old, decaying gristmill located adjacent to Forsythe Road on the river's south side in Anne Arundel County (which became Howard County in 1851). Nearby, on the other side of the river in Baltimore County, he built a large hotel for railroad travelers and summer vacationers.

By 1845, the gristmill had become the Howard County Cotton Factory. Over the following decade the factory became an impressive enterprise employing about 200 workers. Although cotton was not grown locally, the factory's location—near the B&O Railroad and between the South's cotton fields and the North's growing textile industry—made it a promising endeavor. Like other textile factory owners, Sykes had mills in Baltimore, Frederick, and Howard Counties; and the mills were adjacent to rivers that provided waterpower. To increase the likelihood of his venture's success,

Sykes employed skilled English tradesmen in his factories. He relied on access to the new B&O Railroad that made it possible to ship goods inexpensively. The business flourished until the late 1850s. After Sykes sold the business in 1857, successive owners operated the factory sporadically for another decade. The building burned in 1905.

The Baltimore & Ohio Railroad. The B&O Railroad's early designers and engineers had little practical experience to apply to their new enterprise. Although small steam-powered locomotives had been developed in England, B&O's railroad engineers did not plan to use them. Rather, they planned to use horses to pull the cars. A horse could pull three cars, weighing a combined 16,200 pounds, at a rate of three to five miles per hour on a road of rails. The smooth rails allowed them to pull about twelve times more weight than they could on the pitted and often boggy dirt roads of the period. Horses were changed every six to seven miles—known as a a relay—and Sykesville became one of the changing points.

The first seven miles of rail from Baltimore to Sykesville were initially constructed of wood. The next six miles, according to John White and Robert Vogel, were "continued in double track, one track laid with the full stone-stringer system, the other with the wood and stringer on stone block system...that was considered a compromise to be replaced later." Nearly all the earlier stone rail was replaced by the mid-1800s, allowing some of the original stone stringers to be put to other uses, such as in the lintels or walls of local buildings. Original stone stringers will be pointed out as we walk through town.

In small communities like Sykesville, anticipation of the benefits of the railroad may have been offset by anxiety over the arrival of workers and their families. The workers who were contracted to build the railroad lived with their families in wooden shanties that were hastily constructed, disassembled, and reconstructed as work progressed down the line.

Balto. & Ohio R.R. 1836.

The little "Grasshopper" (#7) represents the earliest type of standard steam power used by the B&O Railroad on the Old Main Line, beginning in the mid-1830s. These engines were designed to operate over the sharp curves that plagued the Old Main Line in the early days. By the mid-1840s they were displaced by engines using more conventional power, but a few remained in shop switching service until the early 1890s, and three are preserved today. Herbert H. Harwood, Jr., Collection.

The havoc they sometimes created when they deforested private land for fuel and wood for their temporary dwellings was well-known. They frequently spent some of their fifty-cents-a-day wages drinking and participated in many drunken brawls.

In June of 1831, the railroad workers went on strike near Sykesville because the contractor who employed them would not pay their wages. Whiskey and no pay proved a volatile mix, and, when railroad officials could not arrive at a satisfactory solution, the workers began destroying the line. They did substantial damage to the track for about nine miles east of Sykesville and planned to blow up the railroad tunnel just below the town. When the Baltimore Sheriff and George Patterson—the "posse"—rode out to squelch the riot, they were met by 135 angry men armed with tools. The men ignored the Sheriff's orders, seized the reins of his horse, and refused to let him proceed. An anxious

message was sent from Sykesville calling out the Baltimore militia. Members of Baltimore's Light Brigade traveled by train most of the way—marking the first transport of American troops by rail—and then marched the last seven miles to Sykesville. At daylight, they surprised the rioters and arrested the ringleaders, bringing the drama to a bloodless conclusion.

In 1831 James Sykes decided to capitalize on the coming of the railroad to Sykesville by constructing a large, four-story stone hotel. Fifty feet across and 74 feet deep, it was built in an L-shape with two-story verandas on its front and side. Situated near the mid-point between Baltimore and Frederick along the Carroll County side of the Patapsco, the 47-room hotel and tavern served as a rest stop for railroad passengers. As technology improved the quality and speed of rail travel, stops at the hotel became less frequent and shorter. Still, through the

The Sykes Hotel. James Sykes, considered Sykesville's founding father, came here to make his fortune. He believed the area's economic potential was great because of the B&O Railroad, the Patapsco River's waterpower for mills, and the town's healthy, highland location 400 feet above sea level. In 1831 he built the largest masonry hotel in Maryland, shown here. Photograph courtesy of the Maryland Historical Society

mid-19th century the hotel served as a popular resort for Baltimoreans seeking escape from the heat, noise, smell, and spread of disease that characterized summer urban life.

Sykes was not the only one to capitalize on the railroad's clearing of the right-of-way. Many farmers used it as a common highway for travel by horse or for driving livestock, particularly where they could follow the route of the original turnpike—today's Old Frederick Road—without paying its tolls, as they could do through Sykesville. When the B&O began using steam locomotives, travelers were warned of the dangers of using the right-of-way, and that trespassers would not be tolerated for safety reasons. **George F. Warfield,** a prosperous Baltimore merchant who established the Groveland Estate near Sykesville in 1834, was outraged at

being called a trespasser and informed the railroad company that he and his neighbors would take their frustrations out on the line itself. The Maryland legislature finally passed measures establishing fines for the unlawful use of the right-of-way, and resistance eventually melted away.

The Springfield Estate. Although small farms were the norm in this part of Maryland, a few large estates were scattered throughout the area. Springfield Estate, a self-sufficient plantation of 3,000 acres, was the most impressive. In 1882 Springfield was described in J. Thomas Scharf's *History of Western Maryland* as "one of the most admirable and complete farming establishments in Maryland. It...contains about two thousand acres of land, fifteen hundred of which in 1870 were under cultivation. It is furnished with a flour-mill, sawmill, and a comfortable country-house, with room enough for the uses of home and the claims of a generous hospitality, with lawns, orchards, and out-houses of every description and variety. It is high, healthy, rich, well watered and wooded....Under the cultivation of Mr. Patterson, Springfield became the most celebrated, and was truly what it should be, the model farm of Maryland."

Springfield's first owner, William Patterson, was one of the wealthiest merchants in Baltimore and a director of the Baltimore & Ohio Railroad. William Patterson gave his son, George, possession of the estate in 1824. Until his death in 1869, George over-saw its transformation into a flourishing plantation. The original log house was turned into a classical mansion, 175 feet wide and 50 feet deep, with pil-lared two-story porches. Patterson alternately farmed corn, oats, and wheat, and the farm was known for its horses and superior Devon cattle.

Like a number of other large farms in the region, Springfield relied on the use of slave labor. The area stretching along the Carroll-Howard County border was home to many slaves; and nearly a third of all Carroll County's slaves, or several hundred, resided in the Freedom District. By mid-century George Patterson owned forty slaves, ranging in age from five months to seventy years, and employed them in the mansion and fields at Springfield. Nearly all the town's most prosperous farmers and businessmen owned slaves. In 1850 James Sykes held ten, Stephen T. C. Brown sixteen, and the Warfield fam-ily at least nineteen. Although many of Sykesville's slaves toiled in the fields and homes, others may have worked at the local hotel and factory.

It has been said that the town may have been a stop on the Underground Railroad. Some runaway slaves traveled to Baltimore, attempting to blend into the city's large free black community. Although a few local residences are rumored to have been depots for the network, no evidence of this has been uncov-ered. But as documented in numerous newspapers and official accounts, many runaway slaves traveled through the county on their way to freedom.

Iron and Copper Mine. An important boost to the local economy was supplied by the nearby iron and later copper ore mine. In 1849 Isaac Tyson, Jr., a well-known metallurgist, opened the Springfield Iron Mine on a portion of Patterson's Springfield Estate. At sixty feet copper ore was discovered, and by the time he died in 1861, the mine had produced in excess of 1,700 tons of copper in addition to iron ore. Iron ore from this and surrounding mines was smelted at the Elba Furnace, a steam and water char-coal furnace located a short distance downstream from Sykesville.

Tyson established the Elba Furnace in 1851. The furnace and Sykes' cotton mill both relied on water-power harnessed through dams, and relations between the two enterprises sometimes were strained. In 1851, during a dry spell that increased tensions, Tyson's wife Elizabeth wrote, "It is a mis-erable neighborhood. All the people hate each other, at least the landed proprietors and even the vestry!" (From the collection of the Maryland Historical Society.)

Despite inconveniences, by 1861 the furnace was producing 4,000 tons of car wheel iron. For about twenty years, Sykesville was a hub of industry: Iron ore was shipped to the furnace through the town, and the smelted iron was shipped along with copper ore by rail to Baltimore.

The 1844 Diary of Isaac Van Bibber. As Elizabeth Tyson's writing reveals, Sykesville's early settlers were passionate and private people, determined to pursue and be successful in their ventures. In 1844, Isaac Van Bibber traveled through Sykesville to col-lect funds for the building of a church in Westminster. The diary he kept of his journey includes illuminating entries about some of the notable people he encountered:

"[On Wednesday, March 6, 1844, at the hotel in Sykesville]...Mr. Garratt [who was keeping the hotel] made his appearance, and in answer to my salutation of 'how he did?' very obligingly gave me an account of all his complaints for the last six months, and then by an easy and perfectly natural transition passed over to a very minute detail of the purchase, wearing out, and final abandonment of a most remarkable overcoat. While he was in the midst of this intensely interesting narration, a black woman entered and said something to him in a low tone of voice, but he proceeded without paying the slightest attention to her communication. It occurred to me that dinner was announced, and I felt very sorry to be compelled to interrupt the story in one of the most thrilling passages, to inquire whether it were not so. On receiving a reply in the affirmative, I proceeded immediately in the direction of the dining room, but Garratt followed so close behind and during the greater part of the meal regaled me with the account of his adventurous overcoat. After dinner, I took a short nap; got into the [railroad] cars about 4 o'clock [bound for Baltimore]....

"[On March 9, 1844, at Baltimore.] Immediately after breakfast I entered the cars, and read and shook and grunted until I arrived at Sykesville. Here I met with Mr. [George F.] Warfield, who very pressingly invited me to come and see him. At the same time I met Mr. Sykes, who gave me permission to put his name down on my subscription list for 10 dollars. Leaving Sykesville I rode immediately to Mr. Patterson's, whom I found at some distance from his house, sitting on a log reading a newspaper. I asked him to read what I had written up on the first page of my subscription book, but instead of doing so, he asked me what it was all about. I told him it related to the building of an Episcopal Church in Westminster, at which he shook his head, saying that he would have nothing more to do with the building of Churches, as he looked upon them as causes of contention in the neighborhood. I then hazarded a few words of expostulation, and told him that I would most gratefully receive anything that was offered. To this he made no reply, pretending to be deeply engrossed with an exquisite representation of some steam cars at the head of one of the columns of the newspaper. Finding his thoughts in such a train, I bid him good morning, and received a very polite salutation in reply, rode away. Thus vanished my golden dream of a handsome donation from the wealthy Mr. Patterson.

"[On Sunday, March 10, 1844, at the Warfield home.] Here, I received a warm welcome, and also three names to my subscription list. Miss Susanna and Wm. Henry sang and chanted; and the old man dwelt upon the reminiscences of by-gone times until he was thrown into a terrible panic, by a little Negro boy getting under a side table, and by

his noises inducing a belief that a ferocious bandit, or, at least, a sanguinary housebreaker, was in the room."

Van Bibber's account, from his Diary in the manuscript collection of the Maryland Historical Society, provides a rare glimpse of some of Sykesville's early residents. His descriptions of their personalities and prejudices transform them into "flesh and blood" people and provides a glimpse of mid-19th century life in and around the town.

The Civil War. The Civil War touched the Sykesville community as it did most communities in Maryland. Men from the area served in both the Union and Confederate armies, and at least a few of Sykesville's free black men and manumitted slaves enlisted in the U.S. Colored Troops. During the war, soldiers from both armies made raids on the town. A unit of General J. E. B. Stuart's Confederate cavalry burned the bridge linking Carroll and Howard Counties, destroyed the railroad tracks, and cut telegraph lines on its way to Gettysburg in 1863. Union troops camping near Sykesville later appropriated the machinery belting from the Howard Cotton Factory to use for shoe soles, temporarily halting production. Fortunately, the area was spared the bloodshed and massive destruction experienced by other Maryland communities.

The Flood of 1868. Just a few years after the war, nature rained down its wrath on the town. In July of 1868, heavy rains throughout the area dumped a reported eighteen inches of water in half an hour and caused massive flooding along the entire Patapsco River valley. Fifty people died, and homes, mills and other businesses were reduced to rubble. Damage was severe from both the torrential rain and the destructive debris that broke through the river's many dams. Nearly every bridge from Mt. Airy to Baltimore was washed away.

At Sykesville, the raging river washed away the hotel, devastated crops, and ruined the general merchandise store of Zimmerman & Schultz. At least twelve houses, some homes of former workers of the cotton factory who had fled with their families to the safer north bank, were destroyed. Elba Furnace was damaged by the floodwaters as well; with the decline in the local mining industries pre-

The Sykesville School and its students in 1894.

cipitated by increased competition, it never reopened. Rail lines were damaged, but within a few days the B&O had reestablished service.

After the waters receded, the town slowly rebuilt on the Carroll County side, with buildings fitting snugly inside the bowl-shaped area above the river.

The 1882 Maryland Directory described Sykesville as follows: "The location is sunny and very healthy. The west branch of the Patapsco River passes here and supplies abundance of water for milling and other purposes. It is a flourishing village, and a large business is done in lumber, lime, coal, fertilizers and general merchandise. It is quite a resort for families of the city, many board at farm houses during the summer. Land sells "at an average of $30 per acre; produces 15 to 35 bus. wheat, 20 to 40 oats, 100 potatoes, 8 barrels corn and 2 tons hay." The description is followed by a brief list of the town's

various proprietors and professionals, including a wheelwright, harness maker, huckster, butcher, two physicians and three general merchandise store owners, among others.

In 1884 the large Sykesville train station was constructed. The Queen Anne style building was designed by E. Francis Baldwin, the architect for a number of B&O railroad stations, including the famous Camden Station adjacent to Oriole Park at Camden Yards in Baltimore. Sykesville's new station, as described by Westminster's *Democratic Advocate,* had "comfortable retiring rooms with water and all the modern appliances." At the time, it was the only depot on the line that had a vestibule in the rear. The Station is now a restaurant, Baldwin's Station & Pub.

Education. Education has always been an important concern of Sykesville's inhabitants. The first school in Sykesville, the Springfield Academy, was organized by members of the Springfield Presbyterian Church in 1838. In 1878 the Springfield Institute was established as its successor on land donated by Frank Brown, with a $5,000 building contribution from Mrs. George Patterson several years later. From 1878 to 1893 the school boasted nearly sixty boarders and day students. The school closed around 1900 because of growing competition from public schools and, though used briefly as a Christian coed day school, eventually was torn down.

Warfield College, a four-year preparatory school (scholastically a high school) was established in 1894 by Susanna Warfield, a devout Episcopalian and education activist. The stone school buildings could accommodate thirty boarders, and in 1898 twenty boys were on its roster. The school sponsored a football team as well as literary and dramatic societies. Classes included German, Latin, and Greek, Sacred Studies, and Greek and Roman History in addition to Arithmetic and English courses.

Public Schools. The State of Maryland created public school boards in 1865, and in 1867 Carroll County passed legislation to establish separate schools for white and "colored" students. Schools were locally controlled, and most monies were spent on primary rather than secondary education. At least one primary school for "colored" children was to be established in each school (election) district, assuming a sufficient number of students to support it.

In 1896, the Supreme Court in *Plessy vs. Ferguson* approved the use of separate school systems for black and white children as long as they were equal in quality. Until the Supreme Court decision of 1954, in *Brown vs. Topeka, Kansas,* the state's mission was to provide separate but equal school systems. Still, as the newspapers of the times attest, equality in practice was neither expected nor intended. A public school for white children was in operation in Sykesville by the 1870s, and in 1891 the local board of education agreed to build a new building because of the older one's dilapidated condition. The new school was likely a two-story, brick structure on Springfield Avenue (near the corner of Jeroby Road). It had four classrooms, a library, and principal's office.

A One-Room Schoolhouse. What was school like in rural Maryland in the early 20th century? In 1920 there were still nearly 1,200 one-room schoolhouses for grades one through seven. Less than one-fifth were considered thoroughly modern, sanitary, comfortable buildings. Few children attended high school. The first high school in Carroll County opened in Westminster in 1899. That year only 6 percent of the white children in the county went to high school. There was no high school for black students.

Russell Shipley. One septuagenarian, Russell Shipley, fondly remembers his school days. His family lived on Route 32 in Sykesville, in Howard County. His father owned a 90-acre farm, where the Stedding Sod Farm is today. He raised wheat, corn, and hay and milked cows. Home was a log cabin. In 1919, when Mr. Shipley was seven, he began classes in the one-room schoolhouse across the road. It was the same school his parents had attended, probably built around 1889. (Today, the schoolhouse still faces the Stedding Farm but has been converted to a residence with light blue siding; its gable end faces the road.) Because Mr. Shipley knew more reading and arithmetic than most first graders, he began school in second grade. In third grade, he learned how to write with pen and ink; the ink was in an inkwell in the desk (ballpoint pens had not been invented) .

Schoolchildren walked to school. Most children's formal education ended with the completion of seventh grade. Some children repeated seventh grade to gain another year of schooling. Most did not, because they were needed to work on family farms. Only a few children attended high school.

Not only did the children walk to school, the teacher did, too. It was some years before Mr. Shipley's teacher, Miss Anna McLean, purchased a car. Miss McLean taught grades one through seven, acted as principal and building supervisor and reported to the county board. The children assisted: Some cleaned the slate boards, some filled and emptied the coal bucket for the stove, while others hauled water for drinking from a nearby well.

The multi-grade schoolroom was about 24 feet by 36 feet and was lit only by daylight. Slate boards were the essential writing tools. There were a few bookcases. There were no bathrooms, but there were two outhouses, one for boys and one for girls. Mr. Shipley was fortunate to be able to attend the just-completed high school in West Friendship when he graduated from elementary school in 1925.

Separate but Equal. A school for black children in Sykesville did not open until January 4, 1904. Board Commissioner John O. DeVries was responsible for purchasing about two-thirds of an acre (132 square perches, or rods, of land) with a well on Schoolhouse Road from local resident and postmaster Asa Hepner for $134. The Board then paid $530.50 for construction of the wooden schoolhouse, also about 24-by 36-feet, with six windows and an elevated porch. The schoolchildren relied on a stove for heat, a well for water, and daylight for light. There were two outhouses.

Carroll County had a reciprocal agreement with Howard County to educate students living nearby but in the other's county. Both counties initially paid $3 to $4 to educate a white student and $2 to $3 to educate a black student. In the early 1900s, white teachers received a base salary of $50 per year for 15 pupils and an additional couple of dollars per year for additional students. Black teachers received less per year. By 1920, in Carroll County, white elementary teachers received $537.85, and black teachers received $431.87 per year.

There was no high school for white students living in Sykesville until 1923. Before then, students had to travel either to Ellicott City (until 1908, it was the only secondary school in the county) or to Mt. Airy. Many traveled by train.

By 1923, students overflowed the town's limited classrooms for primary grades, and some classes met in portable units or in a commercial building on Main Street. Construction began on a new elementary and high school for grades one through eleven in the early 1930s, and for a while students attended both schools. In 1936 the new, larger school was completed, and eventually the old one torn down. The new building served until it burned down in April of 1957; it was replaced by a new building in January 1959. In 1968 it was converted into a middle school, and more recently it was considerably enlarged.

The county's first and only black high school, Robert Moton High School in Westminster, named after a well-known black educator, opened in 1925. The county did not fund a bus to transport black children to Robert Moton High School until the late 1930s. It served black students throughout the county from 1925 until 1963, when county schools became fully integrated. Some black students in Carroll County began attending white schools in 1955. Sykesville admitted its first black student in 1959.

The black school on Schoolhouse Road closed in 1938, when many smaller schools were consolidated. Until integration in the late-1950s, black students attended Johnsville Primary School in Eldersburg.

In a less affluent age, the typical rural school building or one-room schoolhouse, whether for white or "colored" children in Howard County, cost less than $800 in 1908. That year the county built two one-room schoolhouses for white children at a cost of $1,581. Until 1916, the state only required children to attend school until age 13.

Today, the black schoolhouse has become a town landmark and important restoration project. In particular the Dorsey family, whose members have been associated with much of Sykesville's history, contributed to this project. The Dorseys moved from Cooksville to Sykesville at the end of the 19th century. They purchased a 41-acre farm, and the family grew, as did the town. Several generations of Dorsey children attended the black schoolhouse. In 1949 Carrie and Edward Dorsey began a tradition of hosting an annual family reunion on Labor Day Weekend. In September of 1999, they celebrated the family's 50th reunion, with more than 110 family members attending. The 1999 reunion was a memorable occasion recognized by Sykesville's mayor, Jonathan Herman, and by letters from Senator Barbara Mikulski and state Senator Larry Haines.

To return to Sykesville's earlier history...

Governor Frank Brown. In 1880 Frank Brown purchased the very large Springfield Estate. The son

Frank Brown, the only Governor of Maryland to call Sykesville or Carroll County home, sold much of his farm to the state for the creation of Springfield State Hospital. The Hospital was the engine of Sykesville's economic growth in the early 20th century. Photograph courtesy of the Sykesville Gate House Museum.

of Stephen T.C. Brown, a noted agriculturist, Frank had grown up on Brown's Inheritance, a large estate that bordered the larger Patterson property. By the time Brown purchased the Springfield Estate, it had earned a reputation as the biggest dairy farm in the area. The estate's mansion and nearly 100 outbuildings, which included a blacksmith shop and gristmill, were enclosed by twelve miles of post-and-rail fences and in many cases could be accessed over improved stone roads.

From 1892 to 1896 Brown served as Maryland's Governor. During his term in office he sold 728 acres of the Springfield property to the state for the establishment of a hospital for the mentally ill. In July of 1896 the facility welcomed its first five patients. The hospital had its own water supply, generated its own power, and met many other of its own needs. In 1908, a three-mile spur off the B&O line, the Dinky Track, was constructed up and around Sykesville to transport materials and coal to the Springfield Hospital.

By 1928 **Springfield State Hospital** sprawled over 1,255 acres and treated nearly 2,000 patients. The facility was, on any given day, larger than the town it bordered; in 1960 it had about 3,375 patients and 1,149 staff. Sykesville's population was only about 1,200 at that time. The facility and the town quickly developed a close relationship, and over the years many people from the surrounding community found employment there. In recent years the Hospital's population has diminished to a few hundred patients as more group home facilities provide custodial care.

The 20th century ushered in new cycles of prosperity and decline for the town. In 1904 Sykesville was incorporated, and the townspeople elected Edwin M. Mellor, Sr., a prominent businessman, as its first mayor. Through the mid-1960s Sykesville was the commercial center for both Carroll's Freedom District and western Howard County. During the first half of the 20th century Main Street was a bustling center of activity. Farm families and townspeople shopped there during the week, but Saturday evening was the time to be seen and meet friends on Main Street. There were many grocery and clothing stores; and people could bowl duckpins, play pool, or see the latest film at the theater on the second floor of the bank building or on the first floor of the northeast dining room of what is now E. W. Beck's Pub. Joyous hellos and tearful good-byes were played out on the train station's platform until passenger service was discontinued in 1949.

Many older Sykesvillians recall the first half of the 20th century with nostalgia, but there were less joyful times as well. In 1913, prohibition split the community, and a tornado touched down nearby, heavily damaging local crops. In 1917 Sykesville sent its sons to war. Some did not return. In 1918-1919, the Influenza epidemic spread fear and death locally as it did throughout the country. The Depression hurt the people of Sykesville; farmland was left idle by farmers who could not afford to plant, notices of mortgagee's sales became common in *The Sykesville Herald,* and, in 1931, the Sykesville National Bank closed its doors, not to reopen for another three years. Six years later a fire heavily damaged several buildings on Main Street. And, in

1941 the town's young men began marching off to fight in the second and largest of the five wars that would mark this U.S. century.

Through it all—good and bad—the community could count on getting the news that mattered most from the local newspaper, *The Sykesville Herald*. In 1913 David W. Dean, Albert M. Hall, and William S. Church, formerly publishers of a Baltimore free newspaper, responded to the promotions and prompting of Wade H. D. Warfield and took the bold step of moving their printing presses to Sykesville. Starting from scratch, the men published the first eight-page issue of *The Sykesville Herald* on September 18th. The enterprise met financial difficulties in its initial years, but in 1918 a stock company was formed by a group of local business and professional people to support the weekly paper.

Frederick Church, the son of William S. Church, spent forty-two years with the newspaper, first in its print shop and later as editor, manager, and owner. In 1971 the newspaper was sold to Stromberg Publishing, then eventually to Landmark Communications. After a brief incarnation as the *South Carroll Herald,* the weekly paper discontinued publication in the early 1980s.

Ironically, changes in transportation that had jump-started the town's original growth later precipitated its economic downturn. In the early 19th century, Sykesville blossomed and thrived because of the railroad. At the same time, the nearby town of Eldersburg laid out by John Welch, who died in 1786, and then by John Elder in 1805, experienced slow and sporadic growth as shipping and long-distance travel by rail outpaced travel by horse and wagon. The end of passenger service on the B&O Railroad in 1949 and the construction of Route 32 bypassing Main Street in the 1960s ushered in a period of stagnation for Sykesville and growth for Eldersburg. The growing trucking industry, the "two-car family," an improved highway system, and nearby malls drew people and dollars away from Main Street. Townspeople were able to travel farther, faster and easier, and many in the area worked, shopped, and spent their leisure time outside the local community. Traditional stores and services could not compete with the prices offered by large department and franchise stores. Sykesville's loss seemed Eldersburg's gain, and the latter's commercial, industrial, and residential growth over the last three decades of the 20th century has been explosive.

Changing Times. For several decades Sykesville businesses bemoaned their fate; many closed their doors, and new businesses floundered or failed. Vacant storefronts and marginal businesses became commonplace. Still, townspeople and surviving business owners did what they could to better their lots and improve the community. A town manager was hired in 1979 to serve as an administrator for the mayor and council. The manager, the mayor and council members planned for growth and development. A new storm drain pipe was installed in the 1970s, ending the summer stench that arose from waste dumped into the open stream running beneath the buildings on the west side of Main Street, as it had been for 100 years. Roads were improved and repaired, parks created, and natural areas landscaped.

In recent years Sykesville has reinvented itself, and the new century holds promise. As the surrounding countryside has changed from sparsely populated farms into prosperous residential developments, the new residents visited the town's specialty shops, convenient restaurants, and professional offices. Once again Main Street came alive. Not with grocery or clothing stores, but with antique stores and a host of specialty services not available at the strip malls. A renewed sense of its own history is manifest in the establishment of a designated Historic District encompassing Main Street and Springfield Avenue. The train station was the first high-profile historic renovation project, and more recently Sykesville partnered with the Maryland Historic Trust to stabilize and restore its turn-of-the-century black schoolhouse. The schoolhouse eventually will be dedicated to local African-American history.

In 1997 the **Sykesville Gate House Museum of History** was established to preserve and present the community's material culture. It is located in the restored Springfield Hospital gate house at the old entrance to the facility on Cooper Drive. With the addition of the Springfield Hospital Museum, the town now boasts three outstanding historic educational sites to serve residents and visitors.

In 1913 Wade H. D. Warfield, E. C. Berry, and George Schrade were leading promoters of Sykesville and its Exhibition in the Lyceum, on the third floor of the Arcade Building, at 7566 Main Street.

In the late 1990s town officials entered negotiations with the State regarding the fate of the vast and now underutilized Springfield Hospital property on the other side of Route 32. In 1999 the town annexed the Warfield Complex, a portion of the property that contains a number of historic buildings. Efforts are underway to attract commercial and industrial enterprises to restore and occupy the structures. Several educational institutions have expressed interest in establishing satellite campuses there. Whether all these plans will be fruitful is as yet unknown, but it is anticipated that new revenues and traffic would fuel Sykesville's latest economic and cultural upswing.

21st Century. Much has changed in and around the town as we enter the new century, but some things remain constant. Sykesville still encourages activities that foster a sense of community and welcome visitors. The June 18, 1881, edition of the *Democratic Advocate* reported, for example, that in Sykesville, "The dull weather of last week was enlivened by many strawberry and ice cream festivals. Nearly all the churches in the neighborhood had one." An annual spring Strawberry Festival at the Gate House Museum still attracts crowds as similar celebrations have done for over a hundred years. In 1913 the Merchants' and Farmers' Carnival Association and the Sykesville Poultry Association claimed in an advertisement for their fall Exhibition at the Sykesville Lyceum (on the third floor of the Arcade Building at 7566 Main Street) that, "All roads lead to Sykesville." It seems they still do each year as the leaves begin to turn. The town's well-attended Fall Festival is a favorite October tradition. Although the farm displays, public speeches, and prizes for the prettiest girl or largest man that were popular in 1913 have been replaced by craft displays, regional and ethnic food, hay rides and, for a brief period, "bed races" down Main Street, the coming together of the community reveals a continuity of spirit.

Neighbors sometimes still quarrel and new growth or unstoppable change can cause brief winces of discomfort, but most residents remember "that certain something" that drew them and keeps them in Sykesville. With emphasis on maintaining its historic flavor and friendly character, Sykesville remains a vital community. Equipped with a special resiliency and eschewing a sleepy image for vibrancy, the town nevertheless has retained its obvious small-town charm.

Sykesville in Winter, early 1900s, as a Baltimore & Ohio passenger train leaves the Sykesville Station on a cold, snowy day. The hill west of the station is surprisingly devoid of trees, compared with today's view. At the turn of the century, trees were a critical resource, providing fuel and building materials, and most hill sides were bare.

MAIN STREET

Let us begin our walking tour at the former B&O Railroad Station, now Baldwin's Restaurant & Pub. Stand on the sidewalk between Southern States and 7615 Main Street, The Nostalgia Shop, and look west toward the Station, one of many designed by Baltimore railroad architect E. Francis Baldwin for the B&O Railroad.

7618 Main Street, Baldwin's Station & Pub. Built in 1884, the Sykesville Station is a typical Victorian building in the Queen Anne style, with red pressed-brick and matching red mortar, sandstone sills and lintels, and a slate roof. Note the extra brick detailing below the cornice. The station has been fashionably and faithfully painted in its original colors of red, chocolate, and sage green, and decorated with spindle-like woodwork; massive wooden brown brackets support a protective overhang on both the south and north sides of

the building. The overhang is not original, but a near replica constructed in 1993.

The Queen Anne style of the building and others in Sykesville comes from England. It features contrasting materials, such as decorative shingles, large medieval-type chimneys, molded decorative bricks, stained glass panes, verandas, balconies, projecting gables and bay windows, and corner turrets in various combinations, creating a picturesque appearance.

In the Victorian tradition, the Sykesville Station offered separate waiting rooms for each sex: Women waited in the room on the left, and men waited in the middle room. The freight room, on the right (west side), had a loading dock and high green wooden doors. In addition, there were a ticket and telegraph office on the first floor and

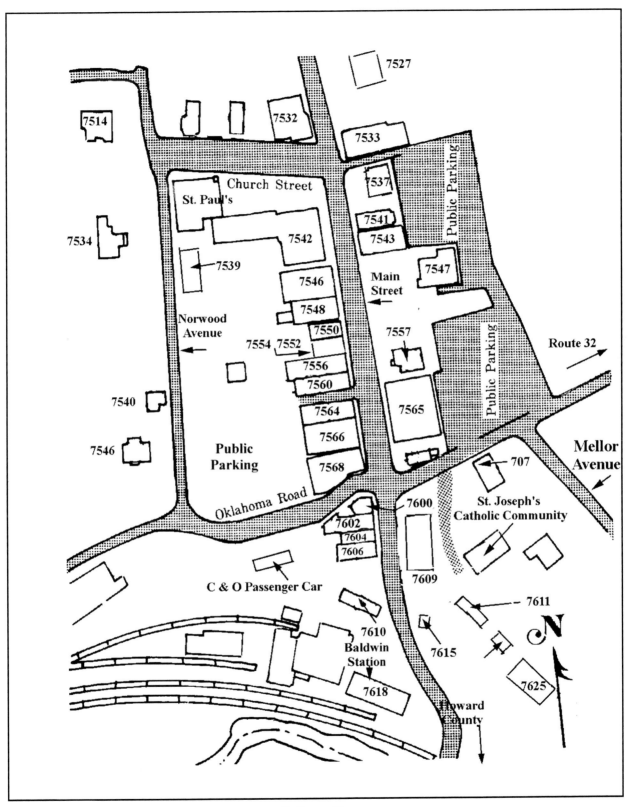

Map 2
Lower Main Street, Sykesville

five small rooms in the small, upper story where the stationmaster and his family lived.

From 1831 to 1948 freight and passenger service was important to the town's economic well-being. Of the two, freight service was more important. The Main Line was periodically improved and rebuilt to handle heavier tonnage freight trains, such as coal trains bringing fuel to Baltimore to be shipped overseas. For most of this period, the station was the hub for area freight and passenger service.

In the early 20th century, with the development of Springfield State Hospital, the railroad's importance to Sykesville expanded. In fact, a separate line was built from the Main Line to the hospital in 1908. Known as the Dinky Line, the spur began west of town, climbed a steep hill to cross Oklahoma Road, and continued across Spout Hill and Springfield Avenue before entering hospital property. It brought fuel, supplies and other materials directly to the hospital. By the 1940s, the hospital could use 60 hopper car loads of coal a month. In 1972 the Dinky Line closed when the hospital converted to using heating oil as fuel.

Farmers and local businesses depended on daily train service to ship or receive produce and products; passengers depended on the railroad to take them to Baltimore or points west. Rail service was the most efficient and comfortable way to travel well into the 20th century.

The national importance of the railroad increased during World War II when trains were used to transport troops and machinery from coast to coast. Years ago, Sykesville resident G. Wilbur Boller described his work for the railroad in 1939. He recalled that the typical week was six days long, or 65.5 hours, and he earned $5.28 a day. Boller remembered that sometimes 18 to 20 trains passed through Sykesville on one eight-hour shift. When this happened, the crew felt overworked. Sometimes, because the track was not maintained as well as it should have been, there were accidents.

On January 22, 1949, *The Baltimore Sun* reported that three trainmen were seriously scalded when 26 cars of a 73-car B&O freight train derailed on a Saturday afternoon in Sykesville. A "section of track broke, pierced the boiler of the engine and was driven back through the fire box into the cab." The article noted the mass of wreckage.

During World War II, with so many men overseas, women went to work for the railroad. When the war ended and life "returned to normal," the role of the railroad changed as its freight-hauling function was increasingly superseded by the trucking industry. Passenger service was affected as well, and in 1949 the B&O discontinued passenger service on the Old Main Line. The station's freight office remained open to handle shipments for the Springfield Hospital Center and other local customers. In the early 1980s, this office closed, and the building was used by CSX Corporation (the present owner of the B&O Railroad) as a maintenance office.

In 1990 CSX sold the Station and mill property to Southern States' Howard G. Crist, who in turn donated the Station to the Town. The Town used public and privately-raised funds to renovate the building and then leased it for a restaurant. Today, the restaurant, Baldwin's Station & Pub, is known for fine dining. Note the wooden addition at the right side of the station. It houses the kitchen and was added when the building's function changed. The kitchen was not built of brick because the State of Maryland required, as a condition for receiving a state grant, that other materials be used to differentiate the new from the original structure. The kitchen's brick red paint assures, however, that the new material blends harmoniously with the old.

Freight trains still travel the line, usually carrying coal from West Virginia to Baltimore, or hauling container boxes from the port of Baltimore to points west.

Behind Baldwin's can be seen Southern States's original silos, grain mills, and storage structures.

7625 Main Street, Southern States Farm and Home Service. The Southern States retail store is an affiliate of the Southern States Cooperative, Inc. (SS), headquartered in Richmond, Virginia. It has offered farm supplies, milled grains, and farming hardware since the late 1940s. The store

In this photograph taken in January 2000, a square white building can be seen on a hill to the left of the station (see arrow). It is one of the original Brown Cottages described on page 70. At the turn of the century, from this spot, the white house on the hill would stand out clearly because there were far fewer trees in between.

was built in 1974 of concrete block and is one of the newer commercial buildings in Sykesville.

Southern States' first buildings were the galvanized sheet metal sheds and milling machines next to Baldwin's Station Restaurant. Before Southern States moved to Sykesville, the business, managed by Frank Dorsey, was at the corner of Liberty Road and Hoods Mill Road. Dorsey moved the business to Main Street in 1947 to gain access to the railroad's freight service.

In the early 1950s, most of Farm and Home Service's business came from local farmers. The railroad was the major transporter of fertilizers, feed, seed, machines and general supplies. When the wheat crop was harvested, railroad cars lined the Sykesville track waiting to be filled. The cars hauled wheat to flour mills, such as the Doughnut Corporation of America in Ellicott City.

In 1951, Howard G. Crist, Jr., resigned as Director of Feed Distribution for Southern States in Virginia and joined Dorsey as a partner. In 1968 he and his wife purchased Dorsey's share of the partnership and incorporated the business.

It was H. Calvin Day, however, who on July 4, 1975, opened the new concrete block facility on the east side of Main Street. Mr. Day began working for Farm and Home Service shortly after graduating from Lisbon High School in 1951 and has managed the Sykesville business with the assistance of his wife Eileen since the 1960s. In 1978 the Crists sold the business to their son Douglas F. Crist, and to the Days.

Since the 1970s Mr. Day and his staff have welcomed more and more suburban families, as more farmland has become new subdivisions. The number and variety of lawn, garden, and seed products has expanded, with an emphasis on organic as well as regular products. In the past, milling was a primary function of the store, but today it is a vestige of a previous time, a convenience for old-time customers.

Today, too, most deliveries arrive by truck. Railroad service is not economical or practical, as it requires exceptionally large orders and an equally flexible schedule. To its credit, Southern States' own manufacturing plants can ship goods on a day's notice.

If you stand in the Southern States parking lot (facing the Southern States building) and look down the railroad track to your right, toward the east, you will see a large, tan-painted brick building, which was built in 1904. The building was previously owned by the State Roads Commission and, before that, by Zimmerman & Schultz, local merchants. *If you walk toward and past this tan building (and under the Route 32 bridge for several hundred feet), you will arrive at the Elba Furnace and Groveland, described on page 10.*

Returning to Main Street and facing the entrance to Southern States, note that the B&O Railroad tracks run parallel to the front of the building. If you look to your left you can see how the tracks in front of Southern States connected to the earlier track alignment, still visible on this side of Main Street and continuing on the west side, behind the office of 7610 Main Street, A Cup Above Coffee Service. Comparing the alignment of the earlier right-of-way with the current CSX track next to the river, you can see how the track has been

The restored station now features Baldwin's Station Restaurant & Pub, which earned a Best New Restaurant award in 1998.

LGB. Lionel Trains, Inc. contributed a fine selection of rolling stock and engines. For information about the club and its hours, call Mark Bennett at 410-795-3157.

The Sykes Hotel. James Sykes' large, imposing, and much celebrated hotel is no longer standing, but we believe it was located opposite the tan warehouse building between the railroad track and the river. Built in 1830-1831, the hotel was impressive for its

straightened and moved away from the buildings. In the straightening process, accessibility to land changed on either side of the track.

The Chesapeake & Ohio (C&O) passenger car was built in 1910 by the Pullman Company as a 28-seat drawing room car. The car houses the toy train collection of the Sykesville and Patapsco Railroad (the S&P RR) and is operated by the Sykesville Model Railroad Club. CSX donated the car through the auspices of John Ott, the former head of the B&O Railroad Museum in Baltimore, and Bruce Greenberg, a local businessman. The S&P RR Club offers an impressive display of model trains including Lionel, HO, N, and

time, measuring 50 feet by 74 feet, four stories tall, and conveniently located next to the railroad and road. From the photograph of the hotel on page 9, we see an L-shaped, stone building covered with stucco, with a low roof and several verandas. The verandas provided welcome cooled ventilation in the summer heat.

The hotel also served as a temporary station and was even used as a house of worship. The small white building in front of the hotel may have also been used as a station. The hotel was ideally situated to accommodate arriving and departing passengers. However, its proximity to the river was a

The C &O passenger car has had many uses. It was initially a drawing room car, later a kitchen car, then a business car, and today it is the home of a model railroad club.

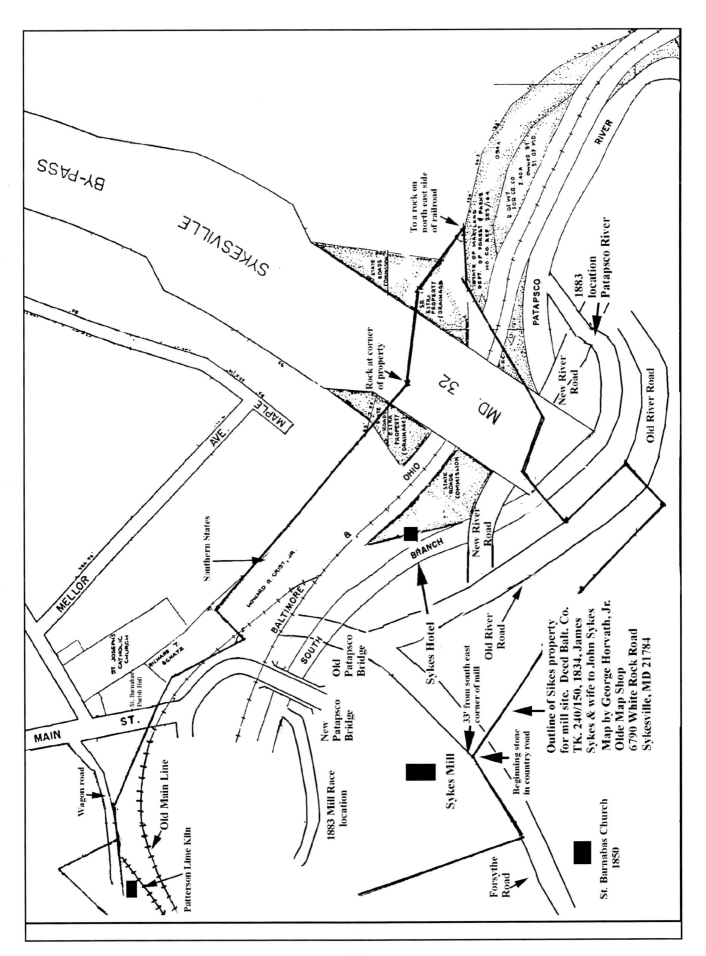

The Sykes Hotel was a grand structure in early 19th century Sykesville. The hotel is in the background (see arrow). This old, well-worn photograph shows the location of the hotel and the track. From this view, we infer that the river is behind the hotel. The photograph also shows a small white building in the foreground that may have served as a railroad station. Photograph courtesy of the Sykesville Gate House Museum.

liability. In the flood of 1868, the hotel was inundated and destroyed.

The 1986 edition of *Sykesville Past and Present* states that the hotel was "on the flat land on the Howard County side of the river." This was based on historical accounts that the town was first developed on the flat Howard County side of the Patapsco River. However, we have verified that there were only a few commercial buildings in Howard County in 1831 as well as in 1868. The most notable buildings prior to 1868 were the mill with millrace, the Zimmerman & Schultz dry goods store, and St. Barnabas Church. Today only two buildings built before 1868 still stand in Sykesville, Howard County: St. Barnabas Church, built in 1850, and a small stone house close to the river.

New Research. Extensive new research suggests that the Sykes Hotel was not in Howard County, as previously thought, but in Carroll County, as described above. (Please see map on previous page.) We base this change in location on the research of Herbert H. Harwood, Jr., railroad historian, who has studied B&O Railroad maps and asserts that this section of track has always been in Carroll County. There are no records of track in Howard County in the area.

In addition, the old photograph of Sykesville reproduced on this page shows the river, the hotel, and the railroad tracks. The question remains, are we looking east or west? Assuming that Harwood is correct, the photographer would have to be looking east in order for the railroad to be on the left and the river on the right. Where was the hotel? Local historian and cartographer George Horvath believes that before the track was straightened out, approximately opposite the tan brick warehouse there was enough space between the river and the tracks for a large building. If the hotel were situated there, it would also explain why the hotel was completely washed away in the flood of 1868.

Additional corroborating information is provided by (1) J. Thomas Scharf's 19th century description of the hotel in relation to St. Joseph's Catholic Church and the railroad in *The History of Western Maryland*; (2) the 1939 letter of Mayor Jones placing early Sykesville a quarter of a mile east of 20th-century Sykesville; (3) conversations with the well-informed Sykesville residents, the Jones sisters, recorded by Jim Purman, Curator, the Sykesville Gate House Museum, placing the hotel near the tan warehouse building; and (4) attempts by the author and Horvath to identify the owners of the parcel of land on which the hotel was built.

Lower Main Street, before 1907, from the vantage point of a passenger arriving in town by train. On the left is a row of stores known as the McDonald Block. The buildings share structural and decorative characteristics, most notably the cornice. Note the last building in the block which is light colored and has a heavy cornice. (See arrow). This building was replaced about 1907 by the First National Bank. The First National Bank building still stands and is now the office of Lloyd Helt (7600 Main). Note the hopper car to the far right on a siding that had been the original Main Line. The Main Line through town was relocated to the south side of the Sykesville Station by 1884.

Most accounts of Sykesville's history, including the first edition of *Sykesville Past and Present*, state that James Sykes purchased 1,000 acres of land from the Patterson family to found Sykesville. Yet when we reviewed actual deeds, indentures, and related legal papers recording land records in Sykesville from 1820 through 1835, no mention is made of James Sykes purchasing land from the Pattersons between 1820 and 1835.

The first mention of Sykes purchasing any land in Sykesville is in 1833. At that time Sykes purchased land from Columbus O'Donnell of Baltimore, a real estate investor or speculator who developed Canton in eastern Baltimore. O'Donnell and Patterson had collaborated on prior land purchases in Baltimore; both were very wealthy men.

Curiously, although Sykesville was named for James Sykes, and Sykes built a large hotel and

summer tourist business, developed a factory and brought workers from England to work in it, and purchased and sold land with the hope of developing the area's economic potential, he was not the earliest or largest landholder of record. If other information becomes available explaining Sykes' relationship to the town's development, we will report it in the *Tour*'s next edition.

Note: The *Census of 1830* for the Sixth District of Anne Arundel County lists the residence of James Sykes on Forsythe, between Eliza Mercer and Henry Griffith.

Now let's return to the east side of Main Street and continue walking up Main Street. The east side of the street provides a better view of most buildings.

7615 Main Street, The Nostalgia Shop, is in front of Schatz's Lawn Mower Service. Today, as for the last twenty or more years, this building has offered a variety of antiques and collectibles.

Before this, it was a small restaurant briefly, and before that a gas station; the pump was between the building and the road. The station had a grease pit, but no hydraulic lift. There is still an open bay in the floor for repairmen to work underneath vehicles. Old-timers remember having their flat tires fixed here. In years gone by, tires punctured easily and frequently, but the inner tubes were repairable.

Sykesville Pumping Station. Sandwiched between Southern States and Schatz's Lawn Mower Service is an important public facility. The small brick building surrounded by wire fence houses the machine that pumps the wastewater from Sykesville (including Fairhaven and Hawk Ridge) to the treatment plant on Arrington Road. After the water is treated, it is released into the Patapsco River. Carroll County Bureau of Utilities built the station in 1976.

7611 Main Street, Schatz's Lawn Mower Service. Frank Dorsey built this two-story building in the early 1940s. In fact, Dick Schatz, the building's current owner, recalls that because raw materials had been requisitioned for the war, Dorsey could not get lumber for his building. Consequently he used cinder block for the first floor and, setting up his own sawmill, cut lumber for the rest of the building. All the timber in the building is rough cut.

Originally, Dorsey's building housed the Wayne Feed and Fertilizer Company. A second building with the same name was nearby, just off Main Street in the parking area of today's Southern States. The second building was severely damaged by Hurricane Agnes in 1972 and no longer exists.

Dick Schatz came to Sykesville in 1969 and began his business across the street, at 7610 Main Street, where A Cup Above is now. When he purchased the building from Dorsey in 1977, it was in sad shape. The steep hill behind the building had given way and a landslide brought down the building's roof. Local contractor Harry Sandosky was hired to repair the building. He suggested using the earth to raise the level of the area next to the building and thereby expand the store's floor space. Sandosky's suggestion worked; the building was repaired and expanded. Schatz opened for business at this location in early 1978.

7609 Main Street, St. Barnabas Episcopal Parish House. This two-story gable-roofed building is a good example of local stonework in the Patapsco River valley. The granite structure is utilitarian, three bays deep and five bays wide on the south end, but only two deep and two wide on the north. It was built in two sections. The larger section, closer to and facing the railroad, was likely built first, and the back, narrower section followed shortly thereafter. The two sections are joined seamlessly on the outside. The building was built by Dr. Orrelana H. Owings as a store for his son-in-law in 1865 and sold to another merchant, John McDonald, in 1868. One of the oldest buildings in Sykesville, it survived the flood of that year.

As a general store in the late 1800s and early 1900s, the stone store sold everything a family of that time needed. On the first floor were barrels of flour, sugar, and salt, as well as underwear, hats, caps, bolts of gingham and muslin for the women, and feed, coal, and tobacco for the men. Loose loaves of bread were not wrapped, but were stacked in wooden crates. Bread was not a big seller because most baking was done at home. Storage rooms were packed with potatoes, coal oil, and feed.

Originally, steep curving steps at the south end led to the second floor. Here, ladies' and men's shoes and boots could be purchased and goods stored.

In 1939, the Volunteer Fire Department purchased and renovated the building. When they moved to a new firehouse up the street in 1949, the building was sold to St. Barnabas for their Parish House. If you look at the stonework on the south end of the building, you will see the cut lines for the firehouse door.

St. Joseph's Catholic Community. Above St. Barnabas Parish House is another stone building. It is St. Joseph's Catholic Church, now called St. Joseph's Catholic Community, Old Stone Church. In 1865 Dr. Owings gave the land for the town's first Catholic church. Until then Mass had been

Lower Main Street, after 1907. A passenger arriving in town by train would note that a wing has been added to the first house to the left of the McDonald Block. (See arrow). It was here (at 7608 Main Street) that Dr. Barnes practiced medicine. To the left is a small wooden building (7610 Main Street) reportedly built as a salt shed in the mid-1800s. It later housed the Sykesville Fire Department. On the right side of Main Street is 7609 which was a store for many years and today is St. Barnabas Parish House.

said in his home. Priests traveled by horse from Ellicott City and Frederick to serve the Catholic families in the area. Baltimore Catholics helped raise money for the new house of worship by selling 25-cent tickets to a concert of sacred music. In 1867 work began, and stone was hauled from Dr. Owings' estate in ox carts. It took some time for the building to be completed. Services began before the roof was in place, and parishioners sat on soap and starch boxes during Mass.

However, the building's structure was not secure. The rear wall collapsed before the roof was completed, and the builder left town, never to be seen again. The church was not dedicated until September 7, 1879. Still, it served as a refuge for people inundated by the flood of 1868.

The church has been improved and renovated through the years. In 1883, a belfry, a gilded cross, and a bell weighing 275 pounds were added. In 1964 and again in 1998 new and much larger churches were built on Liberty Road. Mass is no longer said in Sykesville on a regular basis. To reach the old Sykesville church, take the path that is to the right of Sykesville Video, 707 Sandosky Road.

7610 Main Street, A Cup Above Coffee Service. This modest, wooden two-story building probably was built in the mid-1800s. According to local lore, it was built as a salt shed, and as such had four walls and a roof, but no solid floor. The B&O's Main Line at one time ran on the building's north side, and the track is visible there today. In fact, the track crosses Main Street and passes between The Nostalgia Shop and Schatz's before being covered over by asphalt. In 1933 the building was in dilapidated condition and vacant.

In 1934 the building was offered to the town by J. Marion Harris for their firehouse. The town accepted, concerned by the destruction from a fire at the nearby Hugg Mansion in July 1933. The nearest fire department was many miles away in Ellicott City. Residents organized a Volunteer Fire Company and a campaign to purchase a 500-gallon pumper truck. Volunteers repaired the building and poured a concrete floor so that the new fire engine could be housed on the ground floor and the second floor could be used as a meeting room. The building remained a firehouse until 1939. Information about Sykesville's first firehouse is on page 57.

7608 Main Street no longer exists. The building was located where the parking lot is today next to 7606 Main Street. The frame structure was destroyed in the fire of 1937; in the 1920s and 1930s, the Swain family lived on the second floor and Dr. Robert L. Swain, a pharmacist, operated a drug store on the first floor. After the Swain fam-

Two Former Fire Stations. A 1943 photograph shows how existing structures were modified for the town's fire department; garage doors were installed in each to house the fire engine. On the left, 7610 Main (partially shown) was used as a fire house from 1934 to 1939, and on the right, 7609 Main (with the large door opening) was used from the early 1940s to 1949. Note the engine to the right of the station and the bare hill behind the stone building on the right. St. Joseph's Catholic Church is completely visible on the hill; today this hill is covered with trees and brush. Photograph by Puzz Brightwell.

ily came the H. A. Barnes family. Dr. Barnes (unrelated to Edward Barnes) practiced general medicine on the first floor and resided on the second floor. Also, on the first floor was Henry Forsythe's food market.

Fire! In October 1937, a fire started in the basement of Henry Forsythe's store. Soon flames shot through the roof and, fanned by a brisk wind, traveled to the adjoining buildings. Fire burned the Jones Carpenter Shop, Keeney's Barbershop and Edward Barnes' Poolroom (7606, 7604, and 7602 Main Street). Valiantly the firemen tried to pump water from the nearby Patapsco River, but mud and silt clogged the hose.

After the fire, Dr. Barnes moved to 7332 Springfield Avenue and continued to practice

St. Joseph's Catholic Community. Another building of local stone, the Church has a plain front facade topped by a cupola, and small vestibule flanked by two Gothic windows. Cupolas and towers were popular additions to buildings in the late 19th century. Construction began in 1867 and was completed in 1879.

Fire! In 1937 a severe fire destroyed the home and office of Dr. H. A. Barnes along with Henry Forsythe's new general store and much of the McDonald Block. The flames would have destroyed more of the town except for the brick walls of the First National Bank (at 7600 Main Street), which stopped the fire. The next photograph shows how the three buildings were repaired after the fire.

The McDonald Block Rebuilt, 1943. The 1937 fire destroyed four buildings on the west side of Main Street. Only three were rebuilt, from left to right, 7606, 7604 and 7602. Each has a different facade and as a group are less attractive than the set of buildings they replaced. Photograph by Puzz Brightwell.

medicine and live there. Henry Forsythe joined forces with A. C. Brown (previously a competitor, as was J. Marion Harris's store up the block). The A. C. Brown Store was in the Consolidated Stationers Building (7568 Main Street).

From the sidewalk in front of St. Barnabas Parish House, look across the street at the row of buildings known as the "McDonald Block."

The McDonald Block. The original McDonald buildings date from 1878. They were built by Sykesville architect J. H. Fowble. In the fire of 1937 the buildings were badly damaged or destroyed. The rebuilt structures bear little resemblance to the 1878 originals. The rebuilt, post-1937 block was photographed in 1943. From the left, 7606 lost its cornice detail, though its shop windows were rebuilt in a traditional style; 7604 was rebuilt as a single story building rather than a two-story building; and 7602 was given mini-dormers.

7606 Main Street, Sykesville Antiques. If you walked into this building at the turn of the century, you could purchase stamps in the Post Office and visit with Postmaster Asa Hepner in the back room. He was appointed a third-class Postmaster when William McKinley was President, from 1897-1901. Before leaving, you could purchase tobacco, cigars or confections (sweets). Sykesville had several confectioneries; today we call them convenience stores. Also, in the same building, Mrs. Hepner sold crochet and embroidery cotton, and there was a small music store.

Asa Hepner was a man of many talents. Prior to 1910, Hepner had been in the brick manufacturing business. One newspaper reported that Hepner was so pleased with his first kiln of bricks that "he carried a hot brick around the village to exhibit it."

In 1910, Hepner, the Postmaster for his fourth term, was described by

The McDonald Block, 1999. Compare the irregular 1943 roofline and the present one. The 1999 photo shows more recent changes: Note the shop windows on the first floor of 7606 (far left building) and 7604's new second floor with miniature attic windows to match its neighbor, 7602, on the right.

the *Democratic Advocate* as a man of business ability, a requisite for meeting the demands of the office of Postmaster. Also, in that year, he was in the real estate business to promote the growth and improvement of Sykesville. In addition, he was a director of the Sykesville Building Association and the Sykesville National Bank, a councilman and mayor of Sykesville, and he worked to make Sykesville an important commercial center.

In 1937 William Mason Jones operated a carpenter's shop on the first floor of 7606. The Edward Barnes Family lived on the second floor. Mollie Barnes worked at the Renehan Applebutter Factory, just across the river. Edward Barnes operated a pool hall at 7602 Main Street. The Barnes had two sons and two daughters; both daughters, Alice Hughlett and Puzz Brightwell, still live nearby. In 1996 the sisters recounted how their home had burned. In fact, the irony of the situation is that Mollie Barnes' sister often had teased her, saying, "I wouldn't be afraid to build a fire in the middle of the kitchen floor, with the firehouse next door."

Mrs. Barnes was working at the Renehan Applebutter Factory. When told of the fire, she left Renehan's for home. As she crossed the bridge, she could hardly believe her eyes: She saw the front of her home crumble away, engulfed in flames. She ran the rest of the way. Unfortunately Alice, who was already outside, had not had time to remove valuables from their apartment, not even her grandmother's wedding ring.

The family's fire insurance policy covered only $300! The fire was reported in *The Baltimore Sun*, and people donated goods to help the family; someone even sent a load of used furniture.

Undaunted, Edward Barnes was back in business by 1940. This time his store was at 7606 Main Street. The poolroom had three pool tables, and the store offered soft drinks, ice cream, cigarettes and an ample display of candy. The store's busiest times were Friday and Saturday evenings. The business closed in 1963.

In the 1930s and 1940s, Puzz recalled, women did not shoot pool, and boys younger than 16 were not welcome. A fifteen-to-thirty-minute game cost ten cents, and if a player did not shoot skillfully and a ball jumped the table, her father would glare disapprovingly at the shooter. Puzz remembers her father as appearing very gruff, and he easily scared her boyfriends.

After 1963, 7606 Main Street was home to Pat Winston's Framing Shop, a church, a restaurant, and Think Oak (now located further up Main Street).

7604 Main Street, A. B. Huddlestun's Fine Art Studio/Portraits. Purkey's Toy Trains is expected to replace the Fine Art Studio in the fall of 2000. Purkey will carry O and Standard Gauge trains and buy and sell new and collectible trains.

From 1933 to 1983, Leroy S. "Happy" Keeney 's Barber Shop was a Main Street landmark. Not only was Happy a skillful barber, but he was Sykesville's mayor and the Chief of the Volunteer Fire Department. The Clarence Hayes family lived in the apartment upstairs until the 1937 fire.

Whenever the fire alarm went off, Happy would leave, even if he was cutting a customer's hair. Customers knew that as soon as he returned, he would finish the cut and not charge for it! If you brought a son or daughter in for a haircut, Happy put a seat across the arms of the barber's chair to raise the child to the proper height. Happy liked raising pigeons in his shop and fishing. If he had no customers it took little coaxing to get him to close the shop and head for the river.

After the fire, Happy Keeney continued to operate his Barber Shop in the front; he and his wife Hilda had rooms behind the barber shop.

7602 Main Street, Craftsman Art Company. In the 1920s and early 1930s, Frank Barnes ran a pool hall on the first floor while he and his family lived on the second floor. In the late thirties, prior to the fire, Frank Barnes's widow, Mame, and her family lived upstairs and Edward Barnes operated the pool hall. After the fire, the building was rebuilt; the Mame Barnes family continued to live on the second floor, while the first floor became the office of Wilbur Wimmer's plumbing business. Today the store on the first floor, Craftsman Art Company, offers fine custom framing.

7600 Main Street, Law Office of Lloyd R. Helt, Jr. Built in the latest style for banks in 1907, by J. H. Fowble, Sykesville architect, the building's large Romanesque arched windows outlined in stone, brick walls, and corner quoins convey strength and order. This contrasts with its decorative window treatment in bright green and yellow. The third floor window treatment is appropriately lighter but replicates the pattern below. Through the lower windows, which provide ample interior light, we look into a two-story lobby.

The large, handsome green metal cornice is decorated with dentils and egg-and-dart details and topped with a brick mini-story.

About 1979 the building was renovated by Harry Sandosky, who added a mezzanine between the first and second floors to create more useable office space. Sandosky also installed air conditioning, and renovated the heating, plumbing, and electrical systems.

7600 Main Street was built for **The First National Bank**, organized by Robert W. Carter and A. F. Arrington in March 1907 with a cash and pledge capitalization of $25,000. The bank opened, according to the 1910 *Democratic Advocate Supplement,* "in the midst of a financial panic" and paid indemnity; it was therefore considered able to weather any financial storm. A. F. Arrington and R. W. Carter were Vice Presidents, W. H. Weer was the Cashier, and there were nine directors. Unfortunately, the bank's history was short; it closed in 1916.

The interior was considered a model for tasteful modern fittings in 1907. It was finished in quartered oak, and the writing desks were adorned with plate glass tops. There was a special room to accommodate ladies.

After the bank closed, the building was used for many enterprises. At one time it housed the telephone exchange on the second floor. Mr. Williams ran a butcher shop here as well. Alice Hughlett remembers her fondness for the pickles in the barrel at the butcher shop. Later it became the C. J. Meadows Drug Store. Then in the 1940s Jim Stewart opened a barbershop on the first floor.

The earliest view up Main Street, before 1907. We see on the left corner, at 7668 Main, the building housing today's Consolidated Stationers and State Farm Insurance. In fact, we see how little the building has changed since 1907. Further up the street is the Union National Bank Building, 7564, and lastly the Warfield Building, 7560. What we do not see is the building between the Stationers and Union National Bank. The Arcade Building (today's Greenberg Building) had not yet been built. Prior to about 1907 two smaller, wooden structures occupied this site.

Unlike today, in the early 1900s raising capital and borrowing money for business start-ups, or financing business growth and individual home building, were much more difficult. How did people invest in the future? One way was through a building association such as the Sykesville Federal Savings Association.

The **Sykesville Federal Savings Association,** previously the Sykesville Building Association (1907-1972) and the Sykesville Perpetual Building Association (1870-1907), was an important Sykesville institution.

The Sykesville Perpetual Building Association was organized by dry goods merchants Zimmerman & Schultz to assist farmers from the surrounding counties in borrowing money. The Association's first meeting was held in their store in the spring of 1870. The Association was char-

tered in 1887 and rechartered and reorganized in 1907, when it became the Sykesville Building Association.

In 1870, the Association auctioned off loans and sold them for a premium as high as 20 percent. This process enabled many farmers to purchase real estate and build their own homes. In 1908 the Association paid shareholders an annual dividend of 6.5 percent, and their office was located in the Mellor Building (presently Consolidated Stationers).

The *1910 Democratic Advocate Supplement* reported that the row of houses on Church Street built by George Schrade, President and Director of the Association, was financed through the Association. The first house in the group, possibly 7532 Main (at the corner of Church Street) was built for $800 and rented for $8 a month. In 1910,

In 1943 the Arcade Building looked just as it did when built, around 1907. Until at least the late 1940s, the Arcade Building had a two-story, open walkway from Main Street to the back entrance. For many years, the third floor had a skylight to provide interior illumination. The skylight was covered by 1935, likely earlier. 1943 photograph by Puzz Brightwell.

17 years later, the rent was increased to $10. The success of the first house enabled Schrade to build other houses. In a little more than seven years, Schrade paid $1,010 to the Association in weekly installments. Of the $1,010 he was compensated $738.40 in rent; his outlay was only $271.60.

In September 1972, the Association opened a branch office on Liberty Road in Eldersburg. In May 1985, the Maryland Savings Share Insurance Corporation crisis led the Association to apply to the Federal Deposit Insurance Corporation (FDIC) to insure its depositors' assets. And, in September 1985, the Association built an office building on land previously purchased to consolidate the Association's two locations.

Since December 14, 1998, the Sykesville Federal Savings Association has occupied a new and larger building at 1321 Liberty Road (Route 26). The Association has remained profitable throughout its history and today is a full service institution with assets worth over $40 million.

At the corner of Main Street and Sandosky Road is a shade tree and convenient bench to view the other three corners. It is also an excellent location from which to take in Sykesville's most ambitious buildings: The two banks; the Arcade Building; and the Warfield Building, built between 1901 and 1907.

The impetus for business expansion in Sykesville at that time was the development of Springfield State Hospital and the area's general agricultural prosperity. The driving force of development was Wade H. D. Warfield, who grew up at the nearby estate Chihuahua, now called Raincliffe, on Raincliffe Road. Wade Warfield was a man with a

The Arcade Building, 1964. A dramatic move: *The Sykesville Herald* printing press was hoisted out when the newspaper moved from Main Street to Springfield Avenue in 1964. Another impressive event was the closing in of the two-story center bay to create more office space sometime between 1946 and 1964. Photograph courtesy of Frederick Church.

mission. His ambition motivated others to strive to build their fortunes and to put Sykesville on the map.

7568 Main Street, Consolidated Stationers and State Farm Insurance. This building was repainted in 1997-1998 to appear as it did in the early 20th century. Its strong colors make its plain exterior more interesting. At that time, the first floor was used for commercial space and the second floor for apartments. The building's location, at the crossroads of Main Street and Oklahoma Avenue, is excellent for retail business. Note that the wing on the south required a jog in the road. The wing was the office of the Sykesville Building Association for the first half of the cen-

tury. Then, as now, the awning helps shade the first floor front windows from the morning sun.

In the late 1800s and early 1900s, **E. M. Mellor's General Merchandise Store**, the largest in town, was located here. It offered clothing, carpets, notions, and shoes, as well as groceries "fancy and staple." Mellor built a lucrative business that expanded from only one room in 1879 to more than 10,000 square feet in less than 20 years. Mellor was active in community life and was mayor of Sykesville for three terms. (Mellor certainly made his mark. Note Mellor Street one block east of Main at Sandosky.)

In 1921 A. C. Brown in partnership with Harry M. Phelps purchased the building, and in 1922 Phelps sold his interest to Brown. The store was then known as A. C. Brown General Merchandise.

After the 1937 fire, Henry Forsythe purchased a half interest in the partnership with A. C. Brown, and the store became Forsythe & Brown. The Forsythe & Brown General Merchandise Store lasted until April 1947, when Celius L. Brown sold his interest to Forsythe. Brown became the Cashier at Sykesville State Bank. The general store continued with different owners until the early 1970s, when Henry Forsythe sold it.

Turning our attention, temporarily, to the other side of Main Street, note the small, red brick building on the corner and the long beige stucco building. Both buildings are owned by the Beck Family: One is a very successful restaurant, E. W. Beck's, and the other their carryout food store.

7566 Main Street, the Greenberg Building. Originally called the Arcade Building, it was designed and built by J. H. Fowble for Wade H. D. Warfield about 1907. Fowble's contribution to the town's architectural heritage is impressive. He designed for his contemporaries, but his buildings weathered the test of time. They still have appeal, are structurally sound, and serve the business community today.

Fowble followed the general design of business arcade buildings, then a popular building style. Typically, an arcade building had a wide center corridor with stores on both sides. Fowble chose a premium buff-colored Roman brick for the front

The Arcade Building, after 1973. In the early 1970s, local contractors Harry Sandosky and Gus Biddinger purchased the Arcade Building, then in very poor condition. They modernized the exterior and installed new electrical, heating, air conditioning, and plumbing systems. The first floor and two-story center front facade were finished in contemporary redwood, later painted light gray. Bruce Greenberg purchased the building in 1987.

facade. It appears that he chose the same Roman brick for the Warfield Building at 7564 Main Street, although the latter building conveys a more utilitarian appearance. Note, also, that a less expensive, more common red brick is used for the building's other three sides, and for the sides and backs of each of the street's major brick buildings.

The Arcade Building is topped with a strong metal cornice, painted dark green. Decorative interest is provided by the brick relief, by keystones over the third floor windows, and the painted panels under the windows.

The building's central arcade connected Main Street and Wade H. D.Warfield's coal and lumber business in the rear. The center was open to the roof, and a glass section in the roof lit the interior. A pyramid-shaped glass skylight is still intact, but

hidden by a modern roof on top and a dropped ceiling beneath.

Wade Hampton DeVries Warfield was very successful as an entrepreneur, developer, politician, and state Senator during the early 1900s. He did things in style: He wore spats and a derby hat and enjoyed the service of a chauffeur. When his first wife died, he married his wife's sister. Always an active member of the community, he was a member of the Board of Directors of Springfield Hospital, and a building there was named in his honor. In the late 1920s and 1930s, he suffered financial setbacks. Some say his speculations in wheat were a major cause of his economic problems.

As a result of Warfield's financial problems, the Arcade Building was sold at foreclosure in August 1927. Clarence R. Clarke purchased the building; he lived on Springfield Avenue and sold Prudential Life Insurance from an office in the southwest corner of the Arcade Building. Clarke also managed the Fireside Gift Shop in the south front side of the building. The Shop sold glassware, china, and photographs color-tinted by the Jones sisters. Their pictures were valued, particularly at a time when color photography was not commercially available.

The Jones sisters, Ida, Fanny, and Elsie, were local celebrities. They photographed people and places and hand-tinted their photographs to make them look realistic. Favorite subjects included picturesque landscapes, still-lifes and local buildings. We are indebted to the sisters for their artistry and photographic record.

Early on, Sykesville's first theater occupied the north side of the third floor of the Arcade Building. The theater, called the Lyceum, was used for community events of note. For example, in 1913 St. Barnabas publicized a "Klondike Ice-cream Social" at the Lyceum. Miss Lizzie Hewitt directed dramas there that featured many local people. Later and for many years, the south side of the third floor was occupied by Masonic organizations, such as the Freedom Lodge, No. 112 AF

The Greenberg Building, 1999. In 1998 and 1999 Bruce Greenberg restored the front facade of the Arcade Building. He removed the 1970s front renovation and reconstructed the original facade using earlier photographs of the building. The center bay of the second floor was rebuilt to harmonize with the bays on each side.

& AM, and Freedom Chapter No. 87 of the Order of the Eastern Star.

Earlier, the Post Office was on the right side, in the front, as you faced the building. Later, the Post Office moved across the street to where E. W. Beck's main dining room is now. It was replaced by Jim Korb's clothing and accessory store.

The Sykesville Herald was important to the developing community. Before the arrival of *The Herald*, events in Sykesville were reported in *The Democratic Advocate*, a Westminster newspaper, or *The Baltimore Sun*. Sykesville's news was of secondary importance when compared with news from Baltimore or Westminster. For these reasons Wade H. D. Warfield was determined to give Sykesville a first-rate newspaper whose focus was the town itself. He recruited David W. Dean, Albert M. Hall, and William S. Church. The first

eight-page edition of the *The Sykesville Herald* was published on September 18, 1913. A subscription cost $1.00 a year, payable in advance. In 1913 the newspaper reported that the massive oak timbers passing through the Sykesville railroad yards were destined for Panama for the construction of the Panama Canal.

By 1918, the newspaper was prospering, and a stock company of local business and professional people was formed to solidify the paper's position. William Church's son Frederick joined the firm and gradually assumed more responsibility.

During the Depression, *The Herald* saved the day for many state workers. President Franklin D. Roosevelt had declared March 6, 1933, a "bank holiday," and the newspaper's job shop was asked to print scrip to be used as money for the payrolls of Springfield and Henryton Hospitals and the State Roads Shop.

Local events made the news as well. On Thursday, April 18, 1957, at 2 a.m. Frederick Church went to bed after laying out that week's edition of the paper. Around 3 a.m. he received a call that **Sykesville High School** was on fire. He rushed to the school and knew he would have to scrap his planned front page and replace it with the fire story. He was barely finished by 8 a.m. when he had to take the copy to the printer in Ellicott City. Frederick Church spent 42 years with the newspaper. In 1971 the paper was sold to Stromberg Publishing and later to Landmark Communications. The newspaper's final edition was dated Wednesday, December 28, 1983. Since then, Sykesville and South Carroll County have lacked a newspaper that reports on local events.

From 1938 until about 1948, the Home Furniture Company occupied the front right side of the Arcade Building, until it moved to a new, larger building on Springfield Avenue. Cross and Rosensteel, clothing merchants, later occupied part of the first floor.

Dentistry. One of the first dentists to practice in the Arcade Building was Dr. J. Fred Waesche, a graduate of the Baltimore College of Dental Surgery. Dr. Waesche was followed by Dr. Tirpak and Dr. Jenkins.

Dr. Waesche had an office on the second floor in the rear for 42 years, from 1895 to 1937. In 1910, the *Democratic Advocate Supplement* described him as a man of high esteem in the community, who worked with such skill that he saved patients from "disagreeable experiences." However, not all of Dr. Waesche's patients felt saved from such experiences. In the 1920s, younger patients such as Russell Shipley recalled dreading the slow-moving, treadle-driven drill that bore into a tooth and created terrible pain. This was before the days of local anaesthetics, such as novocain, and high-speed, electric-powered drills.

In 1947 Mabel A. C. Necker and her husband purchased the Arcade Building from Clarence R. Clarke. Next, Harry Sandosky and Gus Bidinger purchased the property and modernized the building and mechanical systems. They sold the building to the National Film & Video Center in 1981. The latter went bankrupt and the bank foreclosed on the property. In 1987 Bruce and Linda Greenberg bought the building at auction to house their growing business, the Greenberg Publishing Company, a specialty publisher of toy train and railroad books for collectors, operators, and railroad enthusiasts. The publishing company worked in tandem with Greenberg Shows, Inc., the sponsor of train and miniature shows, to promote the toy train, miniature and toy hobbies. Both businesses grew and in 1990 they employed over 40 people. In 1991 Kalmbach Publishing of Waukesha, Wisconsin, the nation's largest toy train hobby magazine publisher, purchased both businesses. Kalmbach moved the publishing activities to Waukesha in 1993, but kept the show business in Sykesville.

Today, the Greenberg Building has a number of office tenants: **Greenberg Shows** sponsors 40 model railroad shows at 25 locations across America as well as train and toy auctions; **Greenberg Properties** rents apartments, stores and offices in Sykesville; **Primerica** sells mutual funds, mortgages, life and long-term care insurance; and **Agans and White** offers roof design services.

7564 Main Street, Union National Bank. This handsome, terra cotta brick building was the most

Sykesville State Bank, 7564 Main Street, after 1959. Modernization was the buzzword of Sykesville business leaders, as it was in communities across the country, in the 1950s and 1960s. The bank, then the Sykesville Bank, was given a new interior and a dramatic new exterior. A large metal grille was placed over the brick exterior. By 1986, community leaders had rethought the image they wished to project. (See photograph, next page.)

decorative of the three Fowble buildings. Built in 1901, it was the first bank building designed and built by the architect in Sykesville. The building features well-developed Romanesque arches; the design was intended to convey strength, durability and progressiveness to inspire confidence in Sykesville's new financial institution. The wide arches reflected the Richardsonian influence in commercial architecture. The bank's brick is the narrower, more expensive Roman type, and its terra cotta color complements the terra cotta relief around the windows. The arches soar two stories to emphasis the height and width of the building. At the same time the arches unify the front facade as do the Corinthian columns. The large plate glass windows on both floors increase the attractiveness of both the exterior and interior spaces. Three gracious outdoor lamps illuminate the

In 1986, the bank, then Union National Bank, under the leadership of Joseph Beaver, sought to revive the bank's traditional, small town service image. In 1988 the metal grille was removed, and the building's stately Romanesque windows and brick facade were restored to their former elegance.

street. Note the 1901 date and name **WARFIELD BUILDING** in terra cotta.

In 1959 A. C. Brown, president of the Sykesville State Bank, sought to give the bank a more progressive appearance. He renovated the interior and modernized the exterior by covering the brick with a contemporary metal grille. The large grill was manufactured and installed by the Stuller Construction Company of Taneytown, Maryland. In 1988 Union National Bank, headquartered in Westminster, bought the building, and its president, Joseph Beaver, a preservationist and community activist, undertook the work of returning the bank's facade to its original appearance.

Union National's predecessors were banks. The first, Sykesville National Bank, was built in 1901

The restored Union National Bank in 2000.

by Wade H. D. Warfield, president and director. Originally called The Sykesville Bank, it sought to stimulate "enterprise and thrift" and "advise and assist young men who have accounts with us." Ladies, too, were offered "every consideration."

The bank was organized as the Sykesville State Bank in 1901 with capital stock of $20,000. There were 164 stockholders and 21 directors, including many Sykesville notables. In 1905 the Bank issued certificates of deposit bearing 4 percent interest and savings accounts with 3 percent interest. According to the *Democratic Advocate*'s *Supplement* for October 21, 1910, the Bank was so successful that in 1907, the Board of Directors declared a dividend of 50 percent and increased its capital stock to $50,000; it was admitted to the national banking system. In 1901 its deposits totaled $26,459; by 1909, $250,919.

In 1930 Sykesville National merged with and into the Central Trust Company of Maryland, of Frederick, Maryland. In September 1931, Central Trust was ordered by the State Banking Commission to close its eleven branches, including the Sykesville office.

This was disappointing news to Sykesville businessmen, such as A. C. Brown. He decided to work to reestablish a Sykesville bank and was instrumental in the planning stages. On August 9, 1934, the Sykesville State Bank opened its doors to the public. A. C. Brown was President, J. Marion Harris was First Vice President, Clarence R. Clarke was Second Vice President, and there were seven directors.

In 1947 A. C. Brown's son, C. L. (Celius), sold his interest in their General Merchandise Store to William Henry Forsythe and became the Cashier at the Sykesville State Bank. Later, C. L. Brown became Vice President and, in 1961, President. In May 1966, his son, C. Todd Brown, joined the Bank as Vice President.

In January 1974, the Bank was acquired by Maryland National Bank. Maryland National continued to operate the bank until January 11, 1988, when it was acquired by Union National Bank of Westminster. In January 2000, Union National was purchased by the Mercantile Safe Deposit & Trust Company.

The main floor of this building has always been a bank. The second floor has had several uses. At one time it was the local movie house; today it is the Carroll County Dance Center. Parents can watch their children dance as they relax at Beck's Restaurant across the street.

7560 Main Street, Sphere Solutions, Inc. An information engineering company, Sphere Solutions provides information systems to business clients. The building was constructed as the headquarters for Wade H. D. Warfield, the man who powered Sykesville's commercial growth in the early 20th century. In 1889, Warfield, just 25 years old, brought his dream of business success to Main Street. He commissioned J. H. Fowble to design and build a worthy structure for his headquarters.

Wade H. D. Warfield, entrepreneur, was responsible for building three of Sykesville's most important buildings: 7566, the Arcade; 7564, Sykesville Bank; and 7560, the Warfield Building. Photograph courtesy of the Sykesville Gate House Museum.

The expensive buff-colored Roman brick is plain but tasteful. The rusticated granite blocks of the first floor provide a strong accent to the buff brick. Additional decoration is provided by vertically placed bricks over the large windows on the two upper floors. The wide tri-part windows have a splayed brick arch with granite keystone and impost block. At the roofline, the fine pressed metal cornice is noteworthy. Again, note the less expensive or common red brick used on the outside walls of both Union National Bank and Sphere Solutions. The many windows on the alley provide a great deal of needed interior light.

Warfield's lumber and coal yard, located behind the building, became one of the largest in the state, due in large part to the development of Springfield State Hospital. Because of the volume of business he conducted with the railroad, Warfield had a siding constructed from the Main Line to bring supplies directly into his yard.

7565 Main Street, today's E. W. Beck's Pub. John Edwin Hood built this general purpose building near the busy intersection of Main Street and Sandosky Road in the early 1920s. Known as the Hood Building, its stucco finish and shingle cap roof were not typical local styles. The building has weathered well with time. It has always been used for commercial space on the first floor and apartments on the second; this pattern, with retail or commercial space at the ground level and apartments above, has been a typical design in older urban areas across America. In this photo of the Hood Building, we see the sign for the United Food Store, owned by Herman Reznick, one of the several grocery stores on Main Street in 1943. To its right was the Post Office and to its left the movie theater. Photograph by Puzz Brightwell.

money in bringing it up to current building standards. They were unable to pay the mortgage, and Union National Bank foreclosed on the property. Union National sold it to Jonathan and Laurie Ann Pfefferkorn, who own it today.

By 1910 Warfield had also constructed a large grain elevator, on the other side of Oklahoma Road, and a flour mill. The flour mill is no longer in business, but in the early 1900s it produced 100 barrels of Cook's Delight flour a day.

7565 Main Street, E. W. Beck's Pub. Two stories, with a stucco finish, the Pub's casual yet neat appearance blends well with the contemporary and older building styles on the street. Built about 1925 by John Edwin Hood, the first floor originally served four separate businesses. If one looks across the building's front facade, it is not difficult to imagine four sections. The second floor has always been apartments.

In 1936 the Post Office moved from the Arcade Building to the Hood

Hopper cars on elevated rails delivered coal and other raw materials to his company's bins and other storage containers.

The Sykesville Lumber, Coal and Grain Company served as Warfield's hardware and supply store and provided storage and office space. Later, its name changed to the Maryland Milling & Supply Company.

Wade Warfield's fortunes declined in the late 1920s, and in the early 1930s, the building was bought by Quincy L. Morrow, a manufacturer of crates and pallets. The building was purchased by Charles B. Mullins in 1989. At that time it had a manually operated freight elevator for moving goods upstairs, but lacked central heat and hot water. The Knights of Columbus purchased the building from Mullins in 1990 and spent considerable

7556 Main Street. In the early 1950s the original house at this location was moved from Main Street to an empty space in the parking lot behind the building. A new, one-story masonry building was constructed by Cross and Rosensteel for their clothing store. In the early 1970s this building was modernized with a Colonial Revival front facade by Doc McDougall for his pharmacy.

7557 Main Street.

Building, where it remained until a new building was built at the corner of Sandosky Road and Route 32 in 1976. From 1973 to 1976 the Hood Building was Ye Old Post Inn; for a brief time it was home to the local Moose Lodge, before being sold to Howard Ferguson, who extensively remodeled the interior and opened a contemporary pub. Ferguson sold the business to Brian and Scott Beck, who together with their father, Ernie, have worked successfully to make Beck's a very popular restaurant.

In 1940, the north end of the building was the Phelps Movie Theater. Later, Lester and Maude Phelps owned the entire building, with the Post Office in the south end, a grocery store in between, and apartments upstairs. Maude Phelps sold tickets to the movie theater for 25 cents each.

7556 Main Street, Think Oak Furniture. Think Oak Furniture sells reproduction oak furniture at attractive prices. Prior to Think Oak, the building was Sykesville Hardware and Rental (1989-1995) and McDougall Pharmacy (1967-1989). Charles B. Mullins owns the building.

Across the street, the walkway from the parking lot behind Beck's to Main Street is new and tastefully finished to join both areas. Note the interesting lamplights, emulating Frank Lloyd Wright designs, on either side of the walkway.

7557 Main Street, Residence. Between Beck's and the grounds of the Sykesville Town House (7547 Main Street) is an attractive brick cottage built in the late Craftsman style. The entrance from the street, through a gate, is accented with an inviting, arched hedge.

Owners Wiley and Claudia Canaan Purkey are fortunate to know the history of their home and to have been able to restore it within the Craftsman tradition.

George Selby, a Sykesville contractor, built the house for Irvin and Charlotte Shipley Buckingham in 1931 at a cost of $4,180. Buckingham sold insurance from a first floor office, while his wife owned and operated the Kut 'N' Kurl Beauty Shoppe on the lower level.

They sold the house and business to J. Steward Bankert, who operated a hair salon there for many years. The Purkeys, the home's third owners, bought the house in 1985. At settlement, they were given Selby's proposal, cost estimate, and blueprints, as they had been given to the Buckinghams when they bought the house.

The Purkeys have restored the building's exterior and interior. Two deluxe features of the exterior are the copper gutters and downspouts. Also note several interesting Craftsman features: The glass panes in the window sash are divided by vertical mullions but no horizontal mullions; the first and second stories are divided by a row of bricks, called a soldier course; and the brickwork in the chimney follows an organic basket weave pattern. Also typical of the Craftsman style are the small stained glass windows on each side of the chimney, and the irregular pattern of the brick facade that gives the brick a hand-made quality.

To see the 1995 addition to the house, a two-story garage and studio in early 1930s Craftsman style, take the walkway from Main Street to the parking lot and look to the left. The addition is an excellent "modern" Craftsman building, down to the last detail.

Returning to Main Street, you can see a park area north of the Purkeys' house which is town property. The gazebo is used for town events or by picnickers.

7554 Main Street, Total Travel. Ron and Andrea Jackson, owners of Total Travel, offer a selection of leisure trips to destinations far and near. This

Main Street Buildings in 1943 showing early and possibly original facades. From the left: 7554, 7552, 7550, 7548, 7546 and 7542. They look of a similar time and place, except for the expanse of the last light-colored, shutterless building on the far right. Today, the first two buildings on the left (Total Travel at 7554 and Jim's Barber Shop 7552) have a modern brick facade with colonial doors and showcase windows. They occupy the first floor of a 19th century wooden building. To the right is the popular Harris Grocery Store, although the front sign reads Harris Dept Store. Today, this building is occupied by the Mission Store and has an enameled metal facade. During the 1950s, colored enamel panels were used to modernize buildings. To its right we see stores with protective awnings keeping out the morning sun. Owned by the Harris Family, they were a department store. Today, Miller's Tax Service and Main Street Dry Goods have offices here; the facade is modern brick painted white. Next door at 7546 was a store with a large covered porch. Today, Consolidated Graphics uses the enclosed upstairs porch for office space. Downstairs, a previous owner replaced the older style windows with new ones. Photograph by Puzz Brightwell.

shop and the barber shop next door occupy the first floor of a traditional frame building built in 1878.

7552 Main Street, Jim's Barber Shop. Jim Wilder's Barber Shop is Sykesville's oldest business, having been at this location since 1969, when Wilder bought the business from an older barber. Not only is Wilder deft with the scissors, but he loves playing bass guitar. From 1975 through 1982 he opened his shop for jam sessions on Friday evenings. If you were on Main Street then, you would hear the sounds of bluegrass or country music wafting down the street.

7550 Main Street, The Mission Store; and 7548 Main Street, Patriot Realtors, MTS Financial, and Main Street By Mail. Charles Mullins, a local businessman, owns 7550 Main Street. Jeanette Miller, a Sykesville resident, owns 7548 Main Street and the realty and financial service businesses. Kim Miller owns Main Street By Mail, a dry goods and sewing products store.

At one time the Harris family owned both buildings. The family ran a grocery store at 7550 and a dry goods store at 7548.

7550 has been modernized with white and black steel panels, but the wooden framework of the past peeks out over the first floor. In fact, the

7554 Main Street, Total Travel, and 7552, Jim's Barber Shop, in 1999. The two bays on the left were added after the original building was completed.

7550 and 7548 Main Street in 1999. On the left, the Mission Store occupies the building once home to the Harris Grocery Store. On the right, Harris Dry Goods was replaced by MTS Financial and Main Street by Mail. When the building was modernized in the 1960s, T-111 siding and modern windows were used on the second floor.

Mission Store's cornice still has its original jigsaw woodwork.

7548 Main Street, whose modern brick facade was recently painted white, has a modern second story facade painted light blue that hides its original structure. Its top cornice is original woodwork with jigsaw cutout designs.

The Harris Department Store sold a range of men's, women's, and children's clothing and accessories. Shoes were always in demand; Norma Ferguson remembers buying shoes for her children here in the 1950s. At that time, salesmen

This photograph, circa 1905, shows the earliest known building at 7546 Main Street, a low, two-story building with a flat roof accented with decorative brackets. (See arrow). Also shown are two of the three principal Warfield buildings on Main Street: 7560, The Warfield Building and 7564, The Sykesville Bank. The Arcade Building at 7566 has not yet been built. Also visible at the far left is the predecessor to the bank building at 7600 Main Street. Photograph courtesy of the Sykesville Gate House Museum.

This photograph, taken after 1907, shows changes to 7546 Main Street, the first building from the right. This building has full first- and second-story porches. Photograph courtesy of Sykesville Gate House Museum.

7546 Main Street continues to change. This is either a new or substantially rebuilt building if compared with the earlier photographs. Both the first and second floors are higher, and a third floor with an end gable roof has been added. Photograph courtesy of the Sykesville Gate House Museum.

The fourth change to 7546 Main Street was undertaken by Wayne Gadow in 1979 and 1980. The second floor porch was converted into office space, and the traditional front was replaced with a modern one.

7542 Main Street, prior to 1907. Street and building maintenance were not priorities when this photograph was taken of the three buildings that comprise W. H. Bennett's General Merchandise Store. Photograph courtesy of the Sykesville Gate House Museum.

checked for a correct fit by using an x-ray machine whose green light revealed the foot's exact position in the shoe. Ferguson also remembers buying tricycles for her two boys at the Hering Hardware Store; in 1960 a 10-inch bike cost $10 and a 12-inch bike cost $12.

Early in the 20th century, before the Harris family became a Main Street institution, 7548 was a pharmacy and sold medicines of all kinds, as well as stationery, toilet articles, cigars, tobacco, postcards, cameras, and Kodak supplies. Messrs. Norton and Swain operated the store; the latter graduated with a degree in pharmacy from the University of Maryland. Swain married Esther Sprecher, the daughter of the town's doctor.

7546 Main Street, Consolidated Graphics, provides printing and specialty advertising services. It also offers wedding, graduation, and other formal invitations. Previously, the building was the Sykesville Variety Store, whose proprietors were

The Rosevear Building, 7542 Main Street, in 1999. A hardware store for many years, the building encompasses three small buildings and an alley. It is likely that W. H. Bennett, its owner in the early 1900s, "wrapped" the small buildings and the alley in siding to create one large store. The different buildings can be identified by studying the windows on the second floor. From the left, the first building consists of the first three matching windows. The fourth window was part of the alley fill-in. The fifth and sixth windows comprise the second building, and the seventh and eighth windows were part of the third building. Today, Alexandra's Attic and All Through the House sell antiques on the first floor, and apartments comprise the second and third floors.

William and Erica Brandenburg, Jr.,. Mr. Brandenburg served on the town council, and Mrs. Brandenburg was the town clerk for many years. This building has a modern facade with contemporary show windows on the first floor and T-111 siding and modern windows on the second floor.

The Rosevear Building: 7542 Main Street, Alexandra's Attic; and 7540 Main Street, All Through the House. Alexandra's Attic offers a huge selection of antiques and old and new collectibles. All Through the House offers antiques, accessories, gifts, and pre-owned furniture, as well as interior design services by Creations by Corrine.

This plain building, covered in light green aluminum siding, appears to be one large building. Its unified facade, however, conceals three earlier

buildings and an alley that were converted into useful retail space over 70 years ago. You can see the four sections by studying the windows on the second floor. From the left, the first three windows match by size and placement and represent the first building. The fourth window stands alone and represents the alley that was filled in. Continuing to the right, windows five and six represent the second building, and the last two windows represent the third building. Four other additions are more difficult to observe.

We do not know which building is the oldest of the three owned by W. H. Bennett. In 1883 Bennett had a modest inventory of general merchandise. By 1910, however, Bennett had 15,000 square feet of retail space, and sold farm equipment, furniture, paper and paint, as well as seed and fertilizer. It was Bennett who created the uni-

7547 Main Street, the Sykesville Town House, was painted in 1999 in an early color scheme after its aluminum siding was removed.

St. Paul's Church after its move from Howard County; it is not known how much of the building was disassembled for the move. The house tower and windmill located of 7514 Norwood Avenue can be seen behind the church. The church's main entrance was on Norwood Avenue. This photograph was taken before 1903. Photograph courtesy of the Sykesville Gate House Museum.

St. Paul's Church, probably shortly after the 1903 additions were made. The J. E. Norwood house and its windmill structure at 7514 Norwood can be seen on the hill behind the church. Photograph courtesy of the Sykesville Gate House Museum.

fied facade and added the projecting ground floor showrooms.

The building and business were sold to Harry DeVries, who lived on Springfield Avenue, and later to DeVries Hering. The business evolved from general merchandise to an all-encompassing hardware business. The Hering family sold the business and building to Russell Hughes, and Hughes sold it to Robert Anderson. By the early

Paul's United Methodist Church in 1985.

St. Paul's United Methodist Church The church is set back from the street with a gracious lawn in front. It is surprising to learn that what is now the front of the church was once the rear. When Main Street became a commercial thoroughfare, the church changed its orientation from Norwood Avenue to Main Street. Harry Sandosky created the attractive park in front of St. Paul's.

Originally, the Methodist Church was on the Howard County side of the Patapsco River, near where St. Luke's Church stands today on Route 32. In 1889, the church was moved to Norwood Avenue. When rebuilt at that time, features such as the cornerstone, bell, and stained glass windows were incorporated into the new structure.

In 1903 two gables were added on each side of the main entrance and tied together with a pent roof. The church's stickwork and deco-

1980s, however, the hardware business was in decline and by 1989, the business had failed. Bruce Greenberg bought the building, that year, created apartments on the second and third stories, and renovated the retail space on the first floor.

Turn your attention again to the other side of Main Street and the newly painted and handsomely restored Sykesville Town House.

7547 Main Street, the Sykesville Town House. This Colonial Revival structure, built around 1863 by Sykesville architect J.H. Fowble, was the home of John McDonald, a successful local merchant, who had bought the stone store at 7609 Main Street in 1868. Today it houses the offices of the town's government. The large home, facing south, has a center front gable and a full-width one-story porch with a smaller center gable.

7543 Main Street in 1999. Built in 1949 to house the Sykesville Volunteer Fire Department, the Department moved to a larger, more central location on Route 32 in 1983. In 1984 Bruce Greenberg purchased the building. In 1996 he replaced the large garage door with showroom windows and central doors. Today, A Touch of Olde sells antiques and Civil War memorabilia on the first floor and the Sykesville Children's Center provides child care services on the second floor.

rative shingles on the gables present a dynamic, interesting facade. In 1930 the church was renovated and remodeled. Sunday school rooms and a social hall were added on the left side. Local artist Richard Bagley painted two large and colorful murals inside depicting the birth and growth of Methodism.

As the Sykesville area attracted more and more suburbanites, the church's services became increasingly crowded. In 1995 a major renovation took place, doubling the worship space, providing access for the handicapped, and bringing the building up to today's safety

Across the street, we see a formstone building whose reason for being is clear: "Sykesville Vol. Fire Co."

7543 Main Street, formerly the Sykesville Fire House, A Touch of Olde Antique Store features antiques and collectibles and specializes in Civil War memorabilia.

On the second floor, the **Sykesville Children's Center**, owned by Sykesville resident Aimee Clime, cares for children from infancy through school age and offers a special supplementary program meeting the criteria of the Maryland Accredited Preschool Program. The Center's hours are 6:45 a.m. until 6 p.m.

The two-story, formstone-faced building, the town's Firehouse for many years, was constructed in 1949. It was the first building in Sykesville designed to be a firehouse. Sykesville's Fire Department, as discussed earlier, had been established in 1933 but had makeshift homes, first in the small building next to Baldwin's (7610 Main Street), and then in the larger building across the street, now St. Barnabas Parish House (7609 Main Street).

The 1949 building was designed by a committee chaired by Edward Grimes. Grimes recalled that the committee specified large clear spaces without poles or obstructions for the engine room on the first floor and the community hall on the second. Heavy steel beams were needed to span the 34-foot width of the building and support the second floor. Fortunately for the committee, the Derby Steel Company of Baltimore had a cancellation of

beams for a bridge. The beams, heavy enough to support a three- or four-story building, were available at a very attractive price. However, the Fire House walls had to be reinforced with heavy block to carry the heavier load.

The Building Committee also discussed the material for the front facade. Some members wanted brick, others formstone, but when the vote was counted, formstone won.

The Fire Department was made up of volunteers. In the 1950s about 6 to 8 men went to a weekday fire and about 12 to 15 men went to a weekend fire. There were no women volunteers. The firemen were summoned by a very loud siren mounted on the building's roof. When the siren sounded, nothing else could be heard. The building, typical of Maryland fire halls, had a large community hall and commercial kitchen on the second floor for community events.

Todd Brown, now a Vice President with NationsBank in Frederick, grew up in Sykesville and graduated from Sykesville High School in 1957. He remembers what he liked to do when the fire siren sounded: Because he knew the regulars who went to a fire, he often found a way to leave school and join the men putting out the fire. If there was a call from Springfield State Hospital, the fire engine sped up Springfield Avenue past the school to answer the call.

The most memorable fire for Todd was the fire that demolished the high school in April of 1957. He remembers the valiant but unsuccessful efforts of the men to extinguish the fire without water for the pumps. The school was badly damaged and costly to rebuild. This loss still did not galvanize support for a municipal water system. A public water system and sewage treatment were not available in Sykesville until 1968, and then the services were imposed by the county government.

Fire even occurred close to home. In February 1969, the station itself caught on fire; the engine room was heavily damaged, and two fire trucks destroyed.

In 1983, after 34 years of service, the firemen voted to close the station and build a larger and

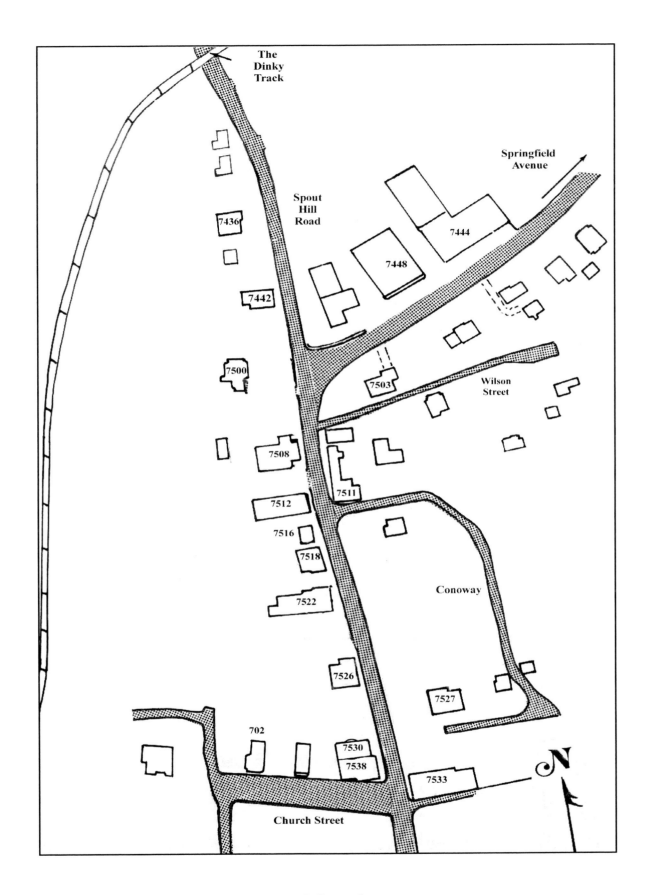

The Dinky Track

Springfield Avenue

Spout Hill Road

7436

7442

7444

7448

7500

7503

Wilson Street

7508

7511

7512

7516

7518

7522

7526

Conoway

7527

702

7530

7538

7533

Church Street

N

Map 4
Upper Main Street, Sykesville

49

7537 and 7533 Main Street. Alvin Howes purchased a British Petroleum gas station at 7537 Main Street in 1974 and converted it into offices for the A. L. Howes Insurance Agency. Its facade is in a Colonial Revival style. 7533 Main Street was rebuilt by Charles Mullins and refinished in a Tudor style on the upper floor. Previously it had been an auto assembly factory, a bowling alley, and a seafood restaurant. Now it is Spaulding Enterprise, a large furniture and home accessory store, operated by Harry and Darlene Spaulding.

more centrally located facility on Route 32 in nearby Flohrville.

In 1984 the fire station was sold to Bruce Greenberg, who renovated the building for business use. In 1996 the large, overhead door was removed and new showroom windows and doors added. To assure the proper finish, a 70-year-old formstone mason was hired to create a new wall that would seamlessly join the old and the new. The mason had worked in the medium for 50 years and promised to "come close."

7541 Main Street, Hair 'N Place. The original brick structure was built about 1900. On the first floor was a popular lunch room and a residence was on the second floor. Today it is a beauty and tanning salon operated by Nicki Swann. Upstairs is an office.

7537 Main Street, A. L. Howes Insurance Agency. A British Petroleum gas station until the late 1960s, this building was vacant for several years before Alvin Howes purchased it in 1974 for his growing insurance business. In 1975 he was given permission to close the bay doors, take out the hoist and level the floor. He opened for business here in 1976.

The Howes Agency was founded in 1953. It provides general insurance for individuals and small town businesses and offers with national financial capabilities. The agency is now owned by Gene Gillispie.

7533 Main Street, Spaulding Enterprise. Today the store sells accessories, furniture, and collectibles. In 1920, cars were assembled in this building. When the dealership ordered Fords from Detroit, sections of the cars were sent by train to Sykesville. When the shipment arrived, men would unload the car parts, put the wheels on their axles, set the bodies into the frames, and tow the cars to the building to complete the assembly. Clyde Dorsey in West Friendship sold the Durant Star, a competitor to Ford. The Star was an inexpensive

Carrollton Apartments, 7530 Main Street. Utilized by the Odd Fellows for many years, today it is an apartment building.

7527 Main, A House with A View, the Lucas House. Local architect, J. H. Fowble, built this large and handsome home for Dr. Frank Lucas in 1907. Extensive excavation was necessary to site the building, and the excavated stone was used to build retaining walls in and around the property. The first floor is distinguished by high ceilings and a bright green tile fireplace surround. As was typical of the times, the doctor's office was on the ground floor, his residence above. Some time ago, the building was divided into apartments.

four-cylinder touring car with a wooden steering wheel and canvas top.

More recent businesses, on the first floor, were a duckpin bowling alley, crab restaurant, and an electric company. The second floor contains apartments.

7532 Main Street, Apartment Building. It is difficult to imagine cars being assembled here and even more difficult to imagine cars being repaired on the second floor, but in the teens, cars to be repaired were hoisted up on a platform by a system of pulleys to be repaired. The cars were Reos and probably Chevrolets. Reos were first made in 1904 by Ransom E. Olds, who had pioneered the Oldsmobile in 1901. The Reo, the initials of Ransom E. Olds, was a durable, quality car, but 1936 was its last year of production.

Other businesses followed. R. Kenneth Barnes Store or Confectionery, was the business most people associate with the corner of Main and Church Streets. On the first floor Barnes had a soda fountain and store where he sold gifts, jewelry, fine watches and tobacco. In addition he was the dealer for Sparton and Philco radios and owned and operated the gas station across the street, where the Howes Insurance Agency is today. In 1940 his nickelodeon and dance floor brought high school students to the store on a regular basis. Barnes' apartment was upstairs. Eventually the building became apartments, and Jim Candeloro purchased the building more recently and improved the apartments.

7530 Main Street, Apartment Building. Now the Carrollton Apartments, this building was known as the Odd Fellows Hall in the late 1800s. The fraternal organization met on the second floor, and various businesses occasionally set up shop on the first floor. For example, Barnes' Confectionary began on the first floor here. The Odd Fellows departed in the mid-1930s, and eventually the building was converted into apartments. The building is owned by Robert Chapman.

7527 Main Street, the Lucas House, Apartment Building. Across the street, high on the hill, is the Lucas Building. It is named for Frank Lucas, general practitioner. Dr. Lucas purchased the lot in 1899 for the significant sum of $500. About 1905 he hired architect J. H. Fowble to build an impressive building. Fowble designed a home with an office, occupying nearly 5,000 square feet on four levels. Built into the side of the hill, its construction involved massive excavation and removal of quantities of rock. The rock was used to build its retaining walls. As was common at that time, the doctor's office was on the ground floor, his residence above. The house was one of the first to have indoor plumbing with running water. A windmill pumped water into a cistern on top of the hill and from there water flowed by gravity into the house. In 1948 the house was sold to Calvin Conaway who divided it into apartments.

Bruce Greenberg, the present owner, would like to find a new owner interested in returning the house to its original glory.

Logs and Chinks. 7526 Main Street is unique in appearance. The log construction on the south and east sides dates it to the mid-19th century. Jazzbo's Dog Grooming occupies much of the first floor. The building's owner, Richard Bagley, is shown completing extensive exterior renovations in 1999. He installed new cedar siding on the building's newer, right side.

7526 Main Street, Jazzbo's Dog Grooming. Partially restored in 1999 by Richard Bagley, the log construction on the house's south and east sides suggests its age; some say it dates to the mid-1800s. One early document mentions William Baer as the owner in 1857, and his name appears at this spot on a military map of 1863. In a log building, the space between the logs is filled with a mixture of sand, lime, and flat stones. Mr. Bagley rechinked and restained the front logs in the fall of 1999.

The north addition was added in the 1880s and doubled the size of the house. It was covered with new shakes in the fall of 1999. A back portion was added between 1910 and 1930. The basement is five feet high and the joists for the first floor are logs that have only one side squared off flat. In addition, the present storefront windows were cut down from the original ones used in the Arcade Building.

The building has served many functions, from Methodist parsonage to general store and town polling center. Sykesville Postmaster Asa Hepner bought the building in 1888. Many years ago Sykesville residents lined up in his parlor to vote.

7522 Main Street. Constructed in 1925 as a garage, it is for sale by its owner, John Serra. Sykesville Auctions is a new tenant.

7518 Main Street, Kevin's Katering. Probably built in two sections, the original building is hidden under its newer brick facing, likely added in the 1960s as part of a revival of Colonial styling. Owner Kevin O'Connor often captures the attention of passersby when he carves large, decorative ice sculptures in front of his building.

In the early 1900s, this house was the home and business of Clarence Brown, one of the three shoe and harness makers in Sykesville. When he needed more space for another business, Brown added a barber chair in his front room. His wife rented rooms to boarders. When the telephone company construction crew was putting up lines in town, she had a full house.

7516 Main Street, Residence. This building has been used as a combination plumbing shop and residence. Later, a barbershop was located on the front, north side.

7512 Main Street, Royal Electric. Royal Electric, owned by Buddy Slack and Skip Edgley,

508 Main Street, formerly Weer Funeral Home. Known •r many years as a funeral parlor, the building today is an apartment building owned by Charles Mullins.

provides well-trained electricians for both new construction as well as repairs and renovations.

When trains brought carloads of new carriages and wagons to Sykesville in the early 1900s, many were destined for this building, R. W. Carter's factory. The light vehicles were stored on the second floor. In fact, there are still double doors high on the backside of the building for easy access to the storage area. The carriages were hauled by pulley up to the second floor. Carter also sold furniture that drew customers from Westminster and Baltimore. About 1920 the building was sold and was converted to a car dealership for Hudson and Essex cars. Hudsons were made from 1909 to 1957. Essex cars were made from 1919 to 1933. The latter is significant because it was the first affordable car to have an enclosed body. Until 1921, most cars were open to the elements; only luxury models were closed. Later, rooms in the building became classrooms when public school space ran out. It was also a sewing factory.

Russell Shipley of Marriottsville has provided interesting early car stories. The Shipleys purchased their first car in 1920. Until then, they drove from their farm on Route 32 to town in a horse and wagon. Mr. Shipley remembers the family's first car. It was a Star made by Durant.

There was a Durant dealership in West Friendship owned by Clyde Dorsey. The Star was an inexpensive four-cylinder touring car with a wooden steering wheel and canvas top.

Along with cars, the Shipleys purchased tractors. Mr. Shipley's father purchased his first tractor in 1924. Mr. Shipley remembers his anticipation of the purchase, particularly his interest in driving and not walking behind the horse to plow the fields. However, when the tractor arrived, it was his father who drove the new tractor. Eventually, Mr. Shipley Senior bought a riding plow for his son. It was advertised as an improved plow because the driver could ride on the plow rather than walk behind it. The plow was purchased at the general store owned by Mr. Bennett on Main Street, in the building that is now the St. Barnabas Parish House. The advertisement did not explain that if the plow's blade hit a large rock, it threw the rider.

7509 Main Street, Apartment Building. In the early 1900s, the butcher was just as important as the grocer. Sykesville residents would make a stop here at the Jenkins Butcher Shop when they were out shopping for the week's groceries.

7508 Main Street, Apartment Building. Now an apartment building, this gray building was once the home of the Weer Funeral Home. In fact it was the second location of the family business, begun in 1888, at 7436 Spout Hill. James Randolph Weer, founder, moved the business closer to the business district. Weer in 1910 was both funeral director and embalmer with the assistance of his son C. Harry Weer. Most bodies were embalmed in a long building behind the funeral home, but occasionally Weer was asked to embalm at the home of the deceased. He performed this service until the 1940s. James R. Weer was also a carpenter. He built the caskets, often of white pine, and covered the insides with gray cloth. C. Harry Weer supplemented the family's income with a small general store in a side room. The Weers lived in the rear of the funeral home. On busy days, they moved the furniture out of the dining room to place bodies on view. Mrs. C. Harry Weer would provide coffee and, occasionally, a ham in the kitchen for visitors.

The Sykesville Hotel, 7511 Main Street, 1912-1913. Hospitality, good food and drink, as well as the latest phone service were features of the Sykesville Hotel at this time. The town's higher elevation helped to make it a cool retreat for city dwellers. Photograph courtesy of William and Rose McDonald.

and we make a special effort to please our guests." "Choice Wines, Liquors, Beers, and Cigars… Bottled Beer for Family Use."

In 1910 the hotel was owned by John Weetenkamp and was described as providing comfortable lodging and a homelike atmosphere for over half a century. In addition to Weetenkamp's good German cooking, guests enjoyed popular Maryland recipes and a well-stocked bar. At that time as well, the front facade of the three-story section was dominated by a wide second floor balcony that created a covered walkway for the first floor. Many Main Street buildings enjoyed balconies until they were modernized after World War II. In a 1912-1913 photograph, the building was painted in a light color with dark shutters. In the last few years, Charles Mullins purchased this building and substantially improved the apartments.

7503 Main Street, **Residence.** In the late 1800s farmers would drive their horses and wagons into these two shops. A blacksmith occupied one shop, a wheelwright the other. Both jutted out into the street at the curve in the lawn.

7500 Main Street, Residence. From the late 1800s until the 1940s Mr. Kohls, a shoemaker, lived here. His home was small, and the central portion was of log construction. His shoe-repair business was in a separate one-room building that is no longer standing. Over the years additions have increased the size of the home. Today this is the home of Charles and Bonnie Mullins.

Continue uphill on Main Street. After you cross Springfield Avenue on the right, Main Street becomes Spout Hill Road.

7442 Spout Hill Road, **Residence.** The retirement home of James Randolph Weer, he lived and died here.

In 1951 the Weers and Haights became partners, and in 1958 the business moved to its present, more prominent location on Route 32 in Eldersburg. Harry Weer Haight and Bryan Luther Haight now own the business. Son Harry Haight describes the Main Street building as looking the same now, except that it was white then. As he recalls, the building was extensively remodeled in the 1930s.

Today, the **Haight Funeral Home** is 111 years old, and the fifth generation of sons and a daughter, Susan Page Herbert, have joined the firm. In 1968 and 1995 the Haights enlarged the facility.

7511 Main Street, Apartment Building. John M. Berry built this hotel after his shop on the Howard County side of the Patapsco River was washed away. It remained a hotel until about 1920 when it became an apartment house. Owner Charles Mullins recently renovated and improved these apartments.

Known as the **Sykesville Hotel**, the building's proprietor in 1905 was Henry Huning. The hotel offered local and long distance C. & P. phone service, SYKESVILLE 8…2. An advertisement in an area directory described the hotel as catering "to the traveling public. Our service is first-class

7436 Spout Hill Road, **Residence.** The first location of the Weer Funeral Home, founded by James Weer in 1888. Weer used the small house to the left to embalm bodies. Behind this house was a two-story building where the horses and hearse were kept. This building no longer exists.

Look up and you will see a bridge spanning Spout Hill Road. The bridge is part of the Dinky Track.

The Dinky Track. In 1908 the State of Maryland laid three miles of track from the Main Line of the B&O to Springfield State Hospital. The railroad spur was requested by the hospital administration so that supplies, particularly coal for the hospital's extensive heating system, could more readily be delivered. From 1908 to 1972 locomotives hauled coal to the hospital on this line, popularly known as the Dinky Track. Sometimes the engines made two or three deliveries a week. The track became obsolete when the Hospital switched its fuel from coal to oil for its heating plant. The trestle over Spout Hill Road and scattered sections of the Dinky Track are reminders of the importance of the railroad and the State Hospital in Sykesville's history. Today, the track's roadbed defines the western side of Sykesville's historic preservation district.

Retrace your steps down the hill to Main Street. Continue to Church Street, just before St. Paul's, and turn right. Church Street ends at Norwood Avenue. Turn left on Norwood Avenue to continue the tour.

Norwood Avenue. Norwood Avenue was originally part of the old wagon road from Sykesville to Frederick, and perhaps consequently, it was early Sykesville's main street because it was situated on the ridge above the wet, swampy area that is today's Main Street. The original firehouse was located here, and St. Paul's Church faced Norwood. The stream that ran down the center of the valley was channeled and the swampy area adjacent to the stream filled in, to create today's Main Street. Eventually St. Paul's turned its

7534 Norwood Avenue. The J. E. Norwood house began as a simple Brown Cottage.

entrance to face Main Street. The road was probably named for railroad agent, J. E. Norwood, whose modest home at 7534 Norwood evolved into a large and elaborate Victorian building.

Today, Norwood Avenue seems narrow, more a lane than the primary route through town. However, several substantial homes were built on Norwood's west side. Builders chose these sites because they provided good views of the valley, fresh water from nearby springs, and well-drained land compared to the marshy land to the east in the valley. Also, just behind Norwood are springs that served as Sykesville's water supply until public water facilities came in 1968. One spring, still privately used, provided water for the B&O steam engines when they were in use.

Many springs originated on Spout Hill, originally called Spring Spout Hill. The water flowed down Main Street in a wooden pipe lined with metal. A watering trough for horses was under the bridge for the Dinky Track.

Springfield Avenue was served by a spring located behind the present middle school. Today these springs are largely captured by the storm water

7546 Norwood Avenue sits on a hill overlooking the town.

drains that run beneath the town and empty into the Patapsco River.

Also, on the steep hill behind these homes was the railroad spur, the Dinky Track, serving Springfield State Hospital.

Two fashionable early homes remain: **7534 and 7546 Norwood Avenue**. Both are handsome examples of local styles as well as adaptations of Brown Cottages. Brown Cottages were built by Frank Brown (prior to his becoming Governor Brown) as rental property for summer vacationers in the 1880s; later he sold them as modest home sites. (Most of the Cottages are on upper Springfield Avenue.) Four were built on this side of Main Street: three on Norwood and one on Oklahoma Road. The cottage on Oklahoma Road is an excellent example of a less modified Brown Cottage; it is nearby, on Oklahoma Road. See a photograph on page 57.

Brown Cottages were plain, with flat roofs, and a center door. They were three bays wide, one room deep, and had a center hall. Today one would never suspect that 7534 Norwood was built as a plain Brown Cottage. It looks more like a Victorian Painted Lady.

7534 Norwood Avenue, **Residence.** In 1886 this home, then a Brown Cottage, was purchased by the Sykesville agent for the B&O Railroad, J. E. Norwood. Norwood had lived in the small apartment provided for the railroad agent over the sta-

tion's waiting rooms. Since the agent had to be available at any time, day or night, he could not live far from the station. The home was purchased by David and Elizabeth Ashman from Jonathan and Becky Herman in 1999.

As we look at this stylish and highly decorative home, we must remember that originally it was a modest and unimproved Brown Cottage. As Norwood's responsibilities increased and he prospered, he rebuilt the cottage to reflect current high style and his improved position. Before the turn of the century, the cottage was "Victorianized": It received a third story with dormers and Mansard roof, a cupola, towers, shingles, a gracious front porch, and an elaborate rear outbuilding. At one time a windmill was atop the tower of the outbuilding. Note the house's eave brackets on the cornice lines and the ornately carved fascia board on the porch.

Square glass windowpanes were popular in the late 19th century, and they too were added to further decorate the facade.

Originally there were two large homes on lots to the left of the Norwood home. Both lots were purchased in the late 1940s by George Henze. Both homes were built as Brown Cottages in the 1880s and were improved before 1900. When asked recently why he bought the corner lot, Henze said he did so because the only access to the middle house was a boardwalk. We have been told that boardwalks connected each house with a central kitchen in the 1880s, when the homes were cottages for summer renters. Unfortunately, both homes were not occupied and became run down-

7539 Norwood Avenue, the site of Sykesville's First Firehouse, jail, and stables.

540 Norwood Avenue.

home, and the corner house, known as the Sprecher House, was demolished many years ago.

Daniel B. Sprecher, M.D., came to Sykesville as a young man in 1881. He lived and practiced medicine here for over 50 years. A doctor, very appreciated by those he cared for, he ministered to the needs of a three-county area and delivered more than 5,000 babies, many of them two generations of the same family.

7546 Norwood Avenue, Residence. In 1996 Jonathan Herman, the mayor of Sykesville, bought and restored 7546 Norwood for his family's residence. As with 7534 Norwood, the Herman's home was built as a flat-roofed Brown Cottage. It was renovated and improved before the turn of the century, when the third story, bay window and other embellishments were added. Today, it is three bays wide, with a hip-shaped standing seam roof and dormer windows.

7539 Norwood Avenue, Residence. When there was a fire in the village in the 1890s, volunteers would rush to this building. If no horses were in the stables, men would grab the tongue of the pump wagon and haul it themselves to the blaze. Strong arms were needed to push the four long handles of the pump up and down. With hard

work, maybe enough pressure could be built up to pump the water ten or twelve feet through a hose. *Walk down the driveway to the rear of the building.*

The stables were located in the lower section of the building next to the jail cells. But horses were kept there only on special occasions such as a town parade.

One section of the building may date back to the mid-1870s. Michael Kasnia, owner and resident here, believes that the oldest area contained a blacksmith's shop from the early 1870s.

In 1905 a chemical fire engine was brought to Sykesville. It was a major event for the small town, and a big celebration was held to hail its arrival.

In the jail section were three narrow cells separated by thick masonry walls, each four and a half feet wide by eight feet long. Initials and the usual jail house humor etched into the walls can still be seen today.

718 Oklahoma Road, a Brown Cottage sits on a hill overlooking the town.

Returning to Norwood and facing the residence, note that the far left section is probably not as old as the right section or fire house. But even here the walls are at least two feet thick. Although the

706 Church Street.

entrance to the fire house is sealed off, the outline of its large doors can be seen on the right side.

Today, the three sections have been remodeled into a handsome private residence.

7540 Norwood Avenue, **Residence.** The original portion of this house was once a stable either for the firehouse or for the residence at 7546 Norwood. It was remodeled as a residence, most likely between 1915 and 1920.

718 Oklahoma Road, **Residence.** This home is an excellent example of an original Brown Cottage. Its characteristic flat roof, square design and plain facade was used many times in Sykesville.

7514 Norwood Avenue, **Residence.** Home of Sykesville architect J. H. Fowble. Not only did Fowble construct buildings for Main Street entrepreneurs, but he built a sizeable three-story frame home for his family. His home is different from the other homes on Norwood in that it exemplifies the Colonial Revival style of the early 20th century. Its asymmetrical projections and ins and outs were considered artistic to contemporaries. The home has a large inviting front porch, cross gables, and a dormer window. Fowble received his architectural training from a correspondence school. By the 1890s he had gained a local reputation as an architect and builder. He designed all of the prominent Main Street buildings, plus other private residences. At Springfield State Hospital he was responsible for the Warfield Cottage, a huge three-story Colonial Revival building with center gable and dormer windows. He also built the two-story dining hall at the Hospital that features a broad, two-story entry porch supported by columns.

706 Church Street, **Residence.** Built in the late 1800s and financed by the Sykesville Building Association (today's Sykesville Federal Savings Institution on Route 26), this row of homes was built by George Schrade. Schrade was President of the Association and practiced what he preached: "The man who owns his own home makes the most desirable citizen as he then has an interest in the community's welfare." The houses on Church Street have rough stone foundations, steeply pitched metal seam roofs, a center Gothic or pointed arched window in the gable, and a center door.

The next four stops on the tour are accessible by car. Please see the map for directions.

Raincliffe, once known as Chihuahua, is located on Raincliffe Road just east of its intersection with Route 32. An elegant, three-story frame res-

Raincliffe on Raincliffe Road.

idence, its facade and interior have changed over time. George Wethered bought Chihuahua in 1856 after he returned from the Mexican War but soon thereafter sold it to Charles A. Warfield. (Warfield was the father of Wade H. D. Warfield, Sykesville entrepreneur.) During the Warfield years, 1862 to 1917, the farm was the second largest dairy farm in the region. The largest was Frank Brown's Springfield.

Chihuahua was always an impressive building, but its appearance has changed dramatically to meet the taste of new owners. The elegant three-story frame building with massive columns was the creation of the Warfields. They enlarged the center section, and the home became a favorite of the many summer boarders who descended on Sykesville to escape Baltimore heat. According to newspaper reports of the 1880s, Chihuahua could house fifty guests. The inside was described as "brilliantly lighted, with soft carpets, rich upholstery and filmy lace curtains."

By the 1930s, the house was sold and remodeled. In 1944 Captain Horace C. Jefferson, owner of the Curtis Bay Towing Company in Baltimore, bought the house. Often referred to as the "dean of the tugboat industry in the United States," he renamed the property **Raincliffe**, after his grandfather's estate in England. Captain Jefferson raised cattle and at one time had one of the largest herds of Hereford cattle on the East Coast. He was also active in Sykesville politics and served as mayor in the late 1960s and early 1970s.

Today, Raincliffe is owned by the State of Maryland. It is being restored through the Department of Natural Resources' private rehabilitation program.

Mill Building. Just north of Sykesville, on the west side of Route 32, is a large white frame gristmill, built in the early 1800s. It has three stories, including a stone basement and large attic. The mill was owned originally by the Patterson Family. In the 20th century and until the mid-1940s, it was owned and operated by DeVries R. Hering. It ground grain, typically flour, chicken feed, cornmeal, and some graham flour, for local farmers. Bonnie Doon flour was ground here and shipped to several East Coast cities. The stone burr or wheel that ground the grains weighs three and one-half tons and is six feet in diameter.

Springfield Presbyterian Church, Spout Hill Road. Built in 1836, the church is an imposing building with three stories of coursed rubble stone covered in stucco, an excellent example of simple Federal architecture. Of rectangular shape, it is three bays wide, with a massive granite stairway

Springfield Presbyterian Church at the top of Spout Hill Road.

leading to the central entrance. A framed doorway and large ten-over-ten sash windows complete the plain but impressive front facade.

The church, the oldest in Sykesville, dates to August 1835 when a group of men met at Brown's Hotel in the village to organize a Presbyterian Church. George Patterson donated land for the site from his Springfield Estate. A number of influential Marylanders have worshiped here, including George Patterson and former Governor Frank Brown. In 1837 the church was incorporated as the First Presbyterian Church of Carroll County. Later the name was changed to Springfield Presbyterian.

In the church vestibule are windows with reveals and plain wood sills and no interior frames. The corner stairway has chamfered posts with a shaped handrail and square spindles. An original church pew with paneled sides is also in the vestibule.

A one-story brick wing was added for educational purposes in 1962. The nave and chancel were remodeled in 1978, and the exterior was painted light gray in 1999. Behind the church is a large cemetery in which are the graves of the Patterson family and other locally prominent community members.

Facing the Church, on the other side of Second Avenue, is the Manse or Parsonage, built in 1856 for the minister. It is still in use today.

St. Barnabas Episcopal Church, 13135 Forsythe Road, Howard County.

The church, a simple, one-story granite building, was built from 1850 to 1851 and has a decorative scalloped verge board (the wide board edging the

St. Barnabas Episcopal Church.

gable-end of the roof), a picturesque belfry, and nine handsome stained glass windows. Four bays deep and two bays wide, when built it had plain glass windows and no belfry. Note the stone blocks with rail indentations from the early B&O Railroad (as you face the church's center door) in the left corner of the granite wall. The stained glass windows were given in memory of Vestryman George Warfield Holmes by his family and friends in the 1880s, and it is believed the belfry was added before 1890. The bell was manufactured in Baltimore. The belfry was rebuilt in 1999 in preparation for St. Barnabas's Sesquicentennial anniversary on June 11, 2000.

St. Barnabas was built because the nearest Episcopal church, Holy Trinity in Eldersburg, built in 1771, was a long ride by buggy for Sykesville residents. The Warfield family, active in restoring Holy Trinity in the 1840s, was also active in petitioning for a local church, called a chapel-of-ease. Susanna Warfield in particular led the campaign to build this church. James Sykes, who had allowed church services to be held in his hotel, favored the idea. Sykes was glad to give land located across from his home for the chapel-of-ease.

The Church of the Holy Trinity no longer exists, but its cemetery does. In the last ten years the cemetery has been resuscitated and cared for by the Friends of Old Trinity Cemetery, under the leadership of Jim Purman, former Caretaker.

Today, St. Barnabas serves parishioners in both Howard and Carroll Counties; and Sunday sermons are preached from the pulpit that once graced the Church of the Holy Trinity.

St. Luke United Methodist Church, Route 32, Howard County.

This is the original site of St. Paul's United Methodist Church before it moved to downtown

St. Luke United Methodist Church.

Sykesville in 1889. The congregation of St. Luke's first met informally in a one room schoolhouse for black children on Schoolhouse Road. Fortunately, St. Paul's was planning to move and donated the vacated land to the congregation and the Norris family. The Norris family and others have remained pillars of the church for three generations and were instrumental in building their own chapel. The church's cornerstone reads "Oct 9, 1898." Restorations and care over the years have kept the church looking new and attracting new members.

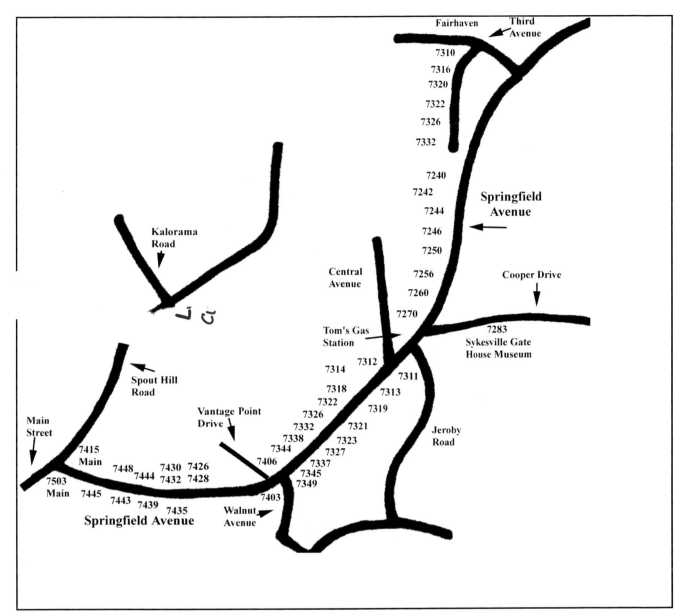

Map 5

Springfield Avenue, Sykesville

SPRINGFIELD AVENUE

Start your walk at the corner of Central and Springfield on the west side of Springfield Avenue, near Tom's Gas Station, and walk down the hill to Main Street.

We do not recommend that you walk north of Central Avenue on Springfield because there is no sidewalk on either side. However, if you drive northward, toward Fairhaven, the road has a wide shoulder where you can park off the road.

A bottle of champagne, music, and speeches marked the opening of Springfield Avenue in 1883. In the early 1880s Frank Brown laid out Springfield Avenue to develop the area for residences. The Avenue was at the western edge of his property which was comprised of the original Patterson Estate that he acquired in 1880, and his family inheritance, the large Brown Estate.

The property line between the Brown and Warfield properties was probably along the north side of Sykesville Middle School. The large Warfield farm bordered Springfield Avenue and extended as far west as Main Street.

7311 Springfield Avenue is located on the east side of the Avenue, at the corner of Jeroby Road. Built in 1895, this typical turn-of-the-century Maryland farmhouse is three bays wide, with a center Gothic roof gable. (The gable is Gothic because of its shape: It has steep sides that meet in a middle point.) This type of house is usually one room deep, although some are larger and have a wing perpendicular to the front facade. Typically, too, the front door is centered under the Gothic roof gable. Inside is a very small landing. The staircase, immediately ahead, divides the first floor into two rooms. Two bedrooms make up the second story.

The exterior has been covered with aluminum siding, except for the third floor, which retains its original fish-scale siding. The stick-style balcony railing on the front porch looks original. The stone foundation is at least 22 inches in width.

The current owners, Craig and Charlie Taylor, bought the house in 1984. They report that the

7312 Springfield Avenue.

house was built as a tenant house for employees of Wade H. D. Warfield, a prosperous farmer and entrepreneur, who owned Chihuahua, a property later known as Raincliffe on Arrington Road. When Warfield suffered financial reversals, he sold Chihuahua, and built the house across the street at 7318 Springfield.

A rear kitchen was added in the 1920s. Also added at that time was an upstairs third bedroom. The house's first bathroom was added in 1976.

7312 Springfield Avenue, is at the corner of Central Avenue. Three bays wide, with a center Gothic roof arch and attic window, this building is deeper than the farmhouse across the street. It is also thought to have been built in the late 1800s, making it one of the older buildings on the Avenue. The house has a rubble foundation, although the porch has a modern concrete block foundation. Its exterior has been covered with siding. It is home today to Bryan and Jamie Tigner.

7314 Springfield Avenue. A postwar prefab, this one-story home, owned by Ralph Brown, sits behind its more imposing neighbor in the front.

7313 Springfield Avenue. Covered with white siding and finished in a more contemporary manner, this house has a new staircase, a black and white striped metal awning, and black shutters.

7318 Springfield Avenue. This property was the last home of Wade H. D. Warfield. According to

7318 Springfield Avenue.

Dorothy Schafer, when Warfield lived here, the grounds looked as manicured as he was. Warfield wore spats and a derby and was driven about town in a chauffeured limousine.

Today the metal roof of the porch is painted black, while that of the house is painted silver. The home's foundation looks reworked. Behind the house, a large imposing garage finished in board-and-batten siding increases the vertical appearance of the structure. The garage's height is also accentuated by the center Gothic gable and the steeply pitched roof.

The house has been reclad in white siding, and it is assumed that the smaller windows were added to the left of the front door.

7319 Springfield Avenue. One of the handsomest houses on the Avenue, 7319 was built in 1891 by George Schrade, President of the Sykesville Perpetual Building Association. The residence appears true to its original structure except for additions in the rear. The house was painted mauve and blue about 1987. It has its original stained wood door with beveled glass, original porch roof supports, and slate steps. Note the original rubble foundation, the fish-scale shingle on the third floor attic gable, and the jigsaw cutout decoration edging the roof line, as well as the slate-like fiberglass shingle roof. Two small bays were added on the south side. Inside is a graceful staircase with a 10-inch-in-diameter newel post. The windows on the staircase landing are stained glass.

7321 Springfield. Square and practical, this style of house is aptly referred to as American Four-

Square. It is a national style seen with regional modifications from coast to coast. Its name derives from its floor plan: Four rooms on the first floor and four on the second. This Four-Square has wooden columns supporting the porch roof. The wood door looks original, and siding covers its original wooden sheathing. Stone steps lead from the concrete walkway to the porch.

7322 Springfield Avenue.

7322 Springfield Avenue. Recently painted, this residence has a replacement concrete porch and a concrete block basement wall. The screened porch enclosing the east end of the house looks original, but the original porch was open. The house's wooden siding was covered some time ago with asbestos shingles. In the attic a wooden ventilation grate replaces a traditional window (as seen on the side of the house). The house's white wooden trim appears intact.

One of the home's first owners was Lester Phelps, owner of the building that is now Beck's Pub (at 7565 Main Street).

7323 Springfield Avenue. Owner Joan Davis looks forward to painting her historic home in the spring of the millenium. The house, an American Four-Square, is 106 years old and has had four owners. Originally, the house was white with green trim and a green shingle roof. Its original bushes, now grown, continue to thrive in front of the wooden porch. The porch has tongue-and-groove construction and flagstone steps. The house's wooden exterior was never covered with siding; its interior boasts hardwood floors.

7332 Springfield Avenue

Previously the home was owned by the George Banks family. In the 1940s and 1950s, Mrs. Banks served dinner to "boarders" weekday evenings. There were usually six guests, mostly teachers from the Sykesville school on Springfield Avenue, who enjoyed her delicious dinners.

7326 Springfield Avenue, Parsonage for St. Paul's Church, Main Street. This appears to be a traditional Colonial home, but it is one of the newest homes on the Avenue. The house was built in 1990 in the Ryland Homes factory and shipped to Sykesville in four sections. Its appearance blends well with its neighbors. Notice the balanced facade, five bays wide, with a center door, and dark green shutters on the light beige siding. The new parsonage replaced its predecessor, which had been condemned due to pesticide contamination.

Between the parsonage and the Queen Anne house next to it on the left, 7332 Springfield, is an asphalt driveway. If you stand in the driveway and look to the west (away from Springfield Avenue), you will see four brick columns on a knoll. The brick columns held a water tank that provided water for the Dinky Track Railroad steam engines that provided service to Springfield Hospital. (The Dinky Track is described on page XX.) The spur carried coal and materials from the B&O Main Line to the Power House at Springfield State Hospital. It stopped at the water tank to take on water. The water was heated into steam, and steam power drove the cylinders that provided the locomotion. Later, when steam engines were replaced with diesels after World War II, the Dinky Track changed to diesel power. The Dinky Track also marks the border of Sykesville's historic district.

7332 Springfield Avenue. This large white, Queen Anne-style home with dark green shutters has a pungent entrance allée of boxwood. Boxwood is a slow-growing shrub, and these, judging from their height, have been here for a long time. The home was built around 1904 for Dr. J. Fred Waesche, a dentist, whose office was in the Arcade Building (7566 Main Street, now the Greenberg Building). He sold the house to H. A. Barnes, M.D., whose office and home on Main Street were destroyed in the fire of 1937. Dr. Barnes lived here and practiced medicine from an office on the north side of the house.

The exterior is wood siding, and the porch columns are original, as is the fish-scale decoration on the attic dormer. The house has a large front bay window and an inviting wrap-around porch. The house is both wide and deep.

7327 Springfield Avenue. The home of the Grimsley Family, this white house set back and sideways is considered one of the oldest houses on the Avenue. It was originally a much smaller building, built of logs and mortar in the late 1800s. It had two rooms downstairs and two rooms upstairs. The downstairs rooms were separated by a staircase. The house has been enlarged over the years.

7331 Springfield Avenue. Owned by Dan and Eloise Stinchcomb, the home was greatly enlarged in 1999. The new addition was tastefully planned to complement the original late 1800s design.

7338 Springfield Avenue. Sharon Kemm, granddaughter of J. Marion Harris, lives in the home her grandfather built in 1930 according to his wife's design. The Colonial Revival style seen here was the fashion in the late 1920s and early 1930s. Stucco, too, was considered a welcome change from the usual wood siding. The crème paint with white trim and black shutters are of that period. Typically, Colonial Revival homes are symmetrical with an equal number of bays on either side of the center door. Sunporches on the south side of the house were considered "a must" at that time.

7338 Springfield Avenue

7344 Springfield Avenue.

J. Marion Harris's father came to Sykesville from Truro, Cornwall, in southern England, an area known for its tin mines. He came to work at the mine on nearby Obrecht Road, but wound up as a very successful grocer and retailer. Mrs. Kemm recalls that her grandfather often helped customers through lean times, that he lent his building next to Baldwin's Station (today's A Cup Above) to serve as a sorely needed firehouse in the early 1930s, and that he was instrumental in helping found the Sykesville National Bank.

7344 Springfield Avenue. Queen Anne in style, this home enjoys a commanding view and considerable shade in the summer from the large trees surrounding it. The white house with its wraparound porch is similar in style and feeling to 7332 Springfield Avenue. Its front bay window is large and inviting.

Built around 1904 by William M. Chipley, the house was occupied by Mr. Chipley only briefly. He sold the house in 1910 after his wife died there in childbirth; he felt he could not return to the home. He later remarried and built a new home at 7321 Springfield Avenue, where he lived for many years. Chipley earned a good livelihood working for Wade H. D. Warfield, but his fortunes declined with those of his employer.

Chipley sold the property to Harry R. DeVries, who owned the large, well-stocked hardware store at 7540-42 Main Street. Mrs. DeVries, known as Aunt Lou, took in boarders, usually schoolteachers, who taught at the school on Springfield Avenue. The DeVries's home offered gracious living, where family and friends enjoyed the spacious lawn and porch in the summertime.

Mr. and Mrs. DeVries lived here until December 1952, when the house was sold to Mr. and Mrs. Bernard Maus. Mr. and Mrs. Maus appreciated the house and entertained often. Mr. Maus had been Superintendent of Grounds at Springfield Hospital. He added the capacious barbecue outside and replaced the old wooden porch with an exact replica. Mrs. Maus is Director of Volunteer Services at Springfield.

7345 Springfield Avenue. William Hepner built this house in 1919, before he built 7349 Springfield. Hepner then moved down the hill and built 7432 Springfield, one of the few stucco homes on the Avenue. Hepner lived there until he died.

Henry Clarke bought 7345 Springfield from Hepner in 1920 and in the 1930s created a landscaped garden in the rear. He then bought the house next door, 7349 Springfield, which Hepner also had built. Mr. Clarke also purchased the house behind, at 7405 Walnut.

7349 Springfield Avenue. This Four-Square home has its original wood siding, a feature that attracted its present owners, the Pattersons. Built in 1921 by William Hepner, it faces Springfield, but its driveway is accessed from Walnut, the corner street. The house is painted a light blue. Its carpentry and that of the house next to it, 7345, share similarities, attributable to the same builder. Note the wide spacing of windows on the second floor and the seemingly narrow front door with a wide window in the first floor facade. The sun porch faces south to catch the sun's warmth in wintertime.

7337 Springfield Avenue as it appeared in 1936.

The entrance to Walnut is marked with two imposing granite pillars, remnants of Sykesville's past. In fact, these posts are made from granite stringers that held the strap rail for the B&O Railroad tracks in 1831. If you look at the stone, you can see some of the grooves for the strap rail. In the 19th and early 20th centuries, these pillars marked one of the entrances to Wade H. D. Warfield's farm and home, Chihuahua. Warfield was one of the landowners who gave Brown permission to build Springfield Avenue. Another set of pillars at Sandosky and Main, now gone, marked another entrance to the Warfield property.

7405 Springfield Avenue. This home was moved to this location from a site on what is now Springfield Avenue. Originally a harness shop, the building was moved and enlarged, and today it is pleasantly typical of the period homes around it. In the 1940s, the Wooden family lived here. Mr. Wooden was the principal of Sykesville High School.

7337 Springfield Avenue. The home is owned by Clarence Clarke's son, Donald, of Devon, Pennsylvania, and daughter, Dorothy Schafer, who lives there now.

Clarence and Norma Clarke purchased the property from Wade H. D. Warfield and built this home in 1924, the year their daughter Dorothy was born. Clarence Clarke, of Scottish-Irish ancestry, sold Prudential Life Insurance. His office was in the Arcade Building, which he then owned. The Clarkes were an established Sykesville family.

The Four-Square style house originally had white window trim, dark green shutters with stained brown shingles on the second floor and attic, and light tan German siding on the first floor. The porch roof is supported by four original tapered wood columns on brick bases. The porch ceiling is painted sky-blue. In 1924 the house had wooden steps, but Mrs. Clarke preferred brick. In 1936 brick steps were installed to replace the wooden ones. Soon, too, the shakes were painted, first in dark green, and then in white. Today the house is covered in white siding and has its original dark green shutters. Note also the widow's walk on top.

Before air conditioning, porches were popular places in the summertime. The glider on the front porch was one of Mrs. Clarke's favorite spots.

Water for the Clarke's home and others on the east side of Springfield was purchased from a well owned by Wade Warfield. Mr. Clarke eventually dug his own well. It was not until the late 1960s that town water and sewage became available.

The Sykesville that Dorothy Clarke Schafer grew up in was like Sykesville today, but was different in many ways. In the 1930s and 1940s, one school building accommodated all grades. The school was on the site of today's **Sykesville Middle School**. In 1940 public school began with first grade and ended with eleventh. Students graduated with either an academic or commercial diploma. English was Dorothy's favorite subject, but her special talent was piano. Dorothy studied piano and her brother Donald studied violin at the Peabody Institute in Baltimore.

On Friday afternoons, and other afternoons as well, popular students from school met at Ken's Confectionery Store, at the corner of Main and Church, where, after buying sodas or ice cream, they jitterbugged to songs such as "Chattanooga Choo Choo" or "String of Pearls" played on the nickelodeon. When they tired, they congregated in the booths to talk and plan weekend activities. Many looked forward to going to the movies. The movie theater occupied the north end of what is now E. W. Beck's Pub (7565 Main Street). Maude Phelps sold tickets, Ted Barnes ran the projector, and admission cost 25 cents.

Some students and their families shopped in Baltimore. The Clarkes shopped at Hutzler's (its

Dorothy Clarke Schafer in 1940.

motto was "Hutzler's is an institution"), or at Hochshield's, or Stewarts on Howard Street, with lunch at the Quixie at Hutzler's or the Oriole Cafeteria. While his family shopped, Mr. Clarke went to Lexington Market to purchase calf's liver and fresh roasted peanuts. Donald and Dorothy did not care for calf's liver but knew they should eat it; and everyone enjoyed the peanuts when they arrived home.

In the summertime, young people sometimes went swimming in one of Sykesville's three "swimming holes" in the Patapsco River. The upstream hole, "the rocks," was for boys only; the hole near the Railroad Station was known for its Sunday afternoon Baptisms; and the hole downstream was known as "the maples."

Sykesville's youth also visited each other, had parties, or attended family and church picnics and strawberry festivals. Churches were known for their special events: St. Barnabas's was known for its Fête of the Lanterns in the summer, and St. Paul's was known for its suppers, dramas, and fall bazaar. Finally, there was the annual Sykesville Fireman's Parade and Carnival.

Dorothy graduated from Sykesville High School in 1940. There were 43 students in the class, and the ceremony took place in the Auditorium of Springfield Hospital. The Auditorium looks the same now as it did when she solemnly marched under rose arches to the platform to receive her diploma. She also learned to drive that year on her father's 1935 Ford.

After graduation, Dorothy went to Western Maryland College to study music for public school teaching. She completed her degree in Music and English, taught music for one year at Sykesville High School, and then went to New York for additional training. She married Bill Schafer in 1945. They lived in the small house on Walnut Avenue next to the Sykesville Apartments. She remembers that in 1945 their rent was $20 a month plus $2 for water. Water was expensive! In 1954 they moved to Woodbine and became the proud owners of an 87-acre dairy farm. For Bill, it was the realization of a life-long ambition. He had always wanted to be a farmer, although he earned his livelihood as a butcher at Lexington Market. Eventually, and after their children were grown, Bill retired to Florida and Dorothy returned to her former home to care for her widowed mother, where she lives today.

7403 Springfield Avenue. This white bungalow, high on the hill, was built around 1925 by Francis Newman, who worked for the Maryland Milling & Supply Company. From the street, the house appears pleasant but modest in size. Its screened front porch obscures the front facade. From the

7403 Springfield Avenue

side, on Walnut Street, the substantial size of the house becomes evident and the white siding with gray-blue shutters gives the building definition. Its driveway entrance is from Walnut, not Springfield.

Inside, the house is spacious with handsome woodwork and a large fireplace. Newman's job provided access to the best lumber and millwork. The bungalow when built, according to Dorothy Schafer, was the only house on the Avenue to be professionally landscaped, and it featured a sunken garden in the rear.

The home's second owners, the DeLashmutts, appreciated the house's style and lavishly decorated its interior with expensive furniture. Mr. DeLashmutt was an established businessman and President of the Woodbine Bank. His wife hailed from Baltimore and was an active civic leader. She founded and served as President of the Women's Club of Sykesville. The Club was affiliated with the Federated Women's Club of America. The DeLashmutts also added the small room at the far end. The third and present owners, the Carrs, rebuilt the porch and enjoy the home's style and panoramic view.

7406 Springfield Avenue. Known today as the Klein House for its owners, Dan and Judy Klein, the house has been continually improved over the years.

Dorothy Schafer's grandfather, John H. L. Clarke, bought this home in 1907. At that time, the driveway was centered at the bottom of the hill and cir-

7406 Springfield Avenue

cled the house from the left. Behind the home was a chicken house and a smoke house, and to the right was a stable, orchard and ice house. The picturesque hill and the entire rock outcropping on the

right front side was known as The Knoll. For some years, from 1907 to 1920, The Knoll was the site of Clarke's blacksmith shop. Later, it served various purposes before being taken down, as were the other outbuildings in the rear. Recently, the Kleins added a large, handsome carriage house behind their home.

There has been considerable discussion among local historians as to the house's original configuration and age. Sykesville mayor and restoration carpenter Jonathan Herman believes the building was one of Brown's original vacation cottages. He noted the silhouetted brackets and fretwork on wood siding now covered with asbestos siding. He also noted how wood scraps were used to cover joints in a way reminiscent of other homes built by Frank Brown in the 1880s.

Local historians believe that the two front rooms (today the living room and dining room) and front entrance and staircase hall were added to the original, smaller building in the late 19th century. The stairs and side door in the back section were probably the home's original staircase and entrance.

Turn right onto Vantage Point Drive. Walk to the top of the street for the best view of the houses there.

Vantage Point Drive

A new street, Vantage Point Drive, was created in 1995 for four new homes which were built in a traditional Victorian style. Each home has a front porch, prominent gables and traditional trim. If you walk up the drive to the high point, you can see the two rear homes. Each presents a good example of a modern interpretation of a Maryland Gothic-style farmhouse, with a well-defined center Gothic gable and a centered arched window. A front porch runs the length of the house, and the front door has lights on each side. The steeply pitched roof completes the design. The colors, too, are bright and eye-catching: One house is tan with maroon shutters, the other light yellow with dark shutters.

Walking back down Vantage Point Drive, we face the past, high on the opposite hill...

7411 Springfield Avenue. A light gray-blue Victorian house with a wrap-around porch and white trim sits at the top of the hill. Its driveway does not connect with Springfield, but with Centre Street, the street behind the house. The house was built around 1920 by John Edwin Hood, who also built the Hood Building (7565 Main Street, now E. W. Beck's Pub).

Between this house and the bungalow at Springfield and Walnut is another tan bungalow. It was built by Herschel Reed but cannot be seen from Springfield Avenue because of the dense bushes and trees in front.

Continuing down Springfield, on the right, are two duplexes built in the 1990s, followed by two manufacturing and sales buildings owned by Dunnrite Casual Furniture. Furniture has been sold in the two warehouse buildings for many years. The warehouses were built by Herman Reznick for his company, the Home Furniture Company, which had offices in the Arcade Building (7566 Main Street, now the Greenberg Building) from 1938 to about 1948. The company moved to a new building next to the gas station on Springfield Avenue. Subsequently, another warehouse-showroom building was built next to the first one.

On the left side of Springfield Avenue are more homes...

7432 Springfield Avenue. Built by William Hepner in the early 1920s, this is one of the town's few stucco-clad homes. Its handsome columns are not original, but are in keeping with the period. They were obtained from a historic house on Route 32, recently demolished, just south of the Haight Funeral Home. At one time, the two doors on the second floor opened onto a sundeck bordered by a low wall. Sundecks were popular features of pre-World War II homes.

7439 Springfield Avenue. A familiar Sykesville style, this white house with dark green shutters has a replacement block foundation, although the wooden porch looks original. Its widely spaced windows and small doors seem characteristic of William Hepner, who built other homes up the Avenue, but in fact the house is not attributed to him. The light brick chimney suggests a later origin.

7443 Springfield Avenue, the Telephone Exchange and *Sykesville Herald* Building. Built about 1920, this two-story brick building was constructed to house the expanding Telephone Exchange. Operators manned the switchboard here around the clock until the phone company

7443 Springfield Avenue

switched to the dial system in 1962. In 1963 the building was sold to Frederick Church, owner of the *The Sykesville Herald*. The newspaper was published from this building until December 28, 1983. Afterwards, Mr. Church operated a printing business here for many years.

7445 Springfield Avenue. A remodeled cottage, it shows the changes that are possible in modernizing and expanding an older house.

7503 Springfield Avenue. At the corner of Springfield and Main, this remodeled cottage has used the site to its advantage: The house has been enlarged over time; the handsome old tree in the front provides shade and character to the property; the fenced area for the dog, the garden and play area, all suggest an active family. Usually unnoticed, Wilson Avenue, a short street, bounds the property on the south side; one of the homes on Wilson Avenue is a Maryland-style farm house.

SPRINGFIELD AVENUE UPTOWN

Starting again from Tom's Gas Station at the corner of Springfield and Jeroby, walk north, or uptown, away from Main Street. The first building of note is the Gate House Museum, located on your right near the corner of Cooper Drive and Springfield Avenue. Beyond the Museum on the

The Sykesville Gate House Museum, 7283 Cooper Drive.

other side of Springfield Avenue is a row of both older and newer homes. The oldest homes are Brown Cottages, built by Frank Brown in the 1880s prior to his becoming Governor of Maryland. An original cottage can be distinguished by its boxy shape and flat roof. Several no longer resemble the cottages they once were because their appearance has changed radically over the years.

7283 Springfield Avenue, The Sykesville Gate House Museum of History. The gatehouse, a compact building of granite, wood and fish-scale shingle, was built as a home for the Hospital's gatekeeper and his family in 1904. Its wide front porch is inviting and hospitable, in keeping with the Hospital's humane philosophy. Note the four impressive stone posts near the house. Until mid-century, they and two other stone posts supported iron gates across the road: The gates were made by the Hospital's blacksmith. Each morning the gate-keeper opened the gates, and each night a Hospital policeman closed them. The policeman made his rounds on a motorcycle with a sidecar.

However, the house was never occupied by a gate-keeper. It was assigned as a residence to various hospital personnel, the most notable being William Shipley, Springfield's Purchasing Agent. He and his wife Lillian raised their two daughters here from 1912 to 1954.

The interior is little changed from 1904. On the first floor, the front door opens into a spacious entrance hall and staircase. To the left is the parlor, to the right the dining room and behind it, a newer kitchen. Upstairs are two small bedrooms.

Originally, the kitchen was located in the base-ment, and the family used a dumbwaiter to bring food up to the butler's pantry. A speaking tube to the basement is still visible and the dumbwaiter still operates. The Shipley girls could play tennis on a double tennis court on the east side of the house. Shipley grandchildren still visit their grand-parents' home and have made significant contribu-tions to the Museum's collection.

At one time, a rose garden graced the backyard and the Dinky Track train rumbled by, frequently pushing as many as six hopper cars of coal to the Hospital's power plant. The tracks can be seen on the embankment just behind the house.

The gatehouse was deeded by the State to the Town of Sykesville in 1995. Restored largely with volunteer labor and donated funds, it is now the Sykesville Gate House Museum of History. The Museum contains a large collection of artifacts, photographs and archival materials. Its curator is James Purman. Museum hours are Wednesdays and Sundays, from 1 p.m. to 6 p.m. and by appointment; the telephone number is 410-549-5150.

Across the street from the Gate House, off Cooper Drive, is the Millard Cooper Park.

Millard Cooper Park. This seven-acre public park has been described as one of the best-devel-oped and -built parks in the state. It is a popular place for concerts, family get-togethers, and out-ings. The Park, the town's first, was named for a town police officer, maintenance superintendent, and friend to many Sykesville residents by an act of the town council in August 1984.

From Jeroby to Third Avenue is a row of homes facing a cornfield, beyond which is Route 32 and Springfield State Hospital. Most of these homes were Brown Cottages when built, although most have been improved or modernized over the years and belie their original design.

Consider, however, the panorama presented in the 1880s photograph of the upper section of Springfield Avenue showing newly built Brown Cottages lined up in a row, without trees or shrubs to distract the viewer. We see countryside without "the country." The cottages appear in pristine con-

An 1880 photograph showing the Brown Cottages.

dition. Today, by comparison, if we look at the line of homes from the north end, near Third Avenue, the panorama includes trees and bushes, driveways, newer homes and cars in a mixture of old and new. At the Third Avenue end, the first home, the Campbell residence at 7210, a tall three-story white building, was once a Brown Cottage. Its owners recently added a third floor to provide more space for their family. In fact, it had been the third cottage in the row; the first two cottages are no longer there.

7250 Springfield Avenue, a Brown Cottage. Perhaps the most original Brown Cottage on Springfield Avenue is this home. It has replacement siding but retains its original boxy shape and flat roof. Interspersed with original cottages on upper Springfield Avenue are newer homes plus improved cottages. The challenge is to figure out what is original, what was added, what is new, and why various changes were made. To gauge the

7250 Springfield Avenue

likelihood and frequency of change, it is instructive to walk through a new development, such as Hawk Ridge off Obrecht Road, and see the range of improvements, additions, and renovations that have taken place to individualize the once-similar building facade within just five years of the development's construction. Realizing the extent of these changes, we can appreciate the possible changes to much older buildings over many years.

For example, in the midst of most of the aluminum- or vinyl-sided buildings is one brick building. When was it built? The present owner, Tim Ferguson, reports that date as 1942. Was it built with its current sunroom? No, the sunroom was a more recent addition, built to complement the style of the home.

Another newer architectural style on Springfield Avenue is the split foyer home with carport. We usually date this style to the late 1960s and early 1970s. Were they built then or later? Were the carports added? Such inquiries can lead to a better appreciation of the homes.

Continue up Springfield Avenue away from Main Street. Turn left on Third Avenue and take an immediate right into Fairhaven.

3700 Third Avenue, Fairhaven, A Life Care Retirement Community. At the intersection of Third Avenue and Springfield Avenue is Fairhaven, an important local institution that employs many local residents. Like Springfield, it was created from the estate of a successful farmer and businessman.

In 1883, the land was part of Frank Brown's Springfield Estate, until it was acquired by Johnzie E. Beasman in 1884. Beasman renamed it Fairfields when he married, and Johnzie and his wife, Laura, began extensive renovations. The small farmhouse became a fourteen-room, three-story mansion. The farmland was used for general farming until Frank, the couple's only son, converted it to a dairy operation. He changed the farm's name to Fairhaven. In the 1930s and 1940s, the dairy farm delivered milk to local customers as well as businesses in Baltimore.

Frank Beasman also owned a construction company and later joined the McLean Construction

Company in Baltimore, where he served as President and chairman of the board. He died in July 1960 at age 71 and left $3,000,000 and over 300 acres of his farm to the Episcopal Church. He asked that the money and land be used for a facility for aged men and women. Fairhaven opened in 1980.

The Beasman Mansion, no longer considered safe by contemporary standards, was torn down. The cost, for example, of adding a sprinkler system and elevator, plus general maintenance costs for the large building, were excessive.

Fairhaven resident Roland Ferguson, a retired forester, established a popular nature trail, planted trees, erected benches and signs, and even uncovered the remains of the old Springfield Iron and Copper Mine. The mine produced iron and later copper from 1849 to 1869. It was reopened for a brief period in 1916 and operated as an open-cut mine for hematite-quartz ore. A note in the Carroll County Historical Society's paper collection states that the shaft extended 2,800 feet underground. The shaft has been covered and only the outlines of the concrete foundations of the operation remain. Nearby, copper tailings cover part of a slope.

Important Facts about Sykesville

1825 James Sykes arrives in what is now Sykesville. The town consists of a saw and gristmill and one or two homes.

1827 Maryland Legislature approves construction of the B&O Railroad.

1831 Sykes replaces old mill with a new one and constructs a 4-story hotel next to the railroad tracks.

1831 B&O reaches Sykesville.

1834 Warfields establish their home at Groveland.

1836 Springfield Presbyterian Church built, Sykesville's first church.

1838 Springfield Academy, first school, opens, operated by Springfield Presbyterian Church.

1845 Sykes opens the Howard County Cotton Factory, employs 200 workers; mill closes in 1857.

1846 Dr. Orrelana Owings, physician, opens practice.

1846 Post office established in the Zimmerman and Schultz Dry Goods Store; J.M. Zimmerman Postmaster.

1847 James W Tyson erects Elba Furnace.

1867 Public schools are organized in Carroll County.

1868 Flood of 1868 inundates Sykesville.

1878 Springfield Institute opens; offers classes to boarding and day students; closes in 1900.

1880 Springfield Estate is purchased by Frank Brown.

1884 Baldwin's B&O Railroad Station opens.

1892 Frank Brown elected governor; serves one term.

1894 Maryland Legislature appropriated $100,000 for a hospital to accommodate insane persons.

1896 State purchases 759 acres for Springfield from ex-Governor Brown for $50,000.

1896 Telephone service operates as a branch of the Ellicott City system.

1899 First year of rural free mail delivery

1904 May 4, the town incorporates as a municipality.

Early 1900s Wade H. D. Warfield, 1864-1935, hires local architect J. H. Fowble to build the Sykesville National Bank, the Warfield Building and the Arcade Building. Warfield was President of the Sykesville Lumber, Coal and Grain Company, later reorganized as the Maryland Milling and Supply Company.

1907 Springfield cares for 740 patients.

1907 Wade Warfield establishes the Sykesville Realty and Investment Company.

1913 Wade Warfield enlists David Dean, Albert Hall, and William Church to publish *The Sykesville Herald*. Last issue is in 1983.

1919 Telephone service moves to the Telephone Exchange Building, 7443 Springfield Avenue

1936 Springfield Hospital cares for 2,600 patients with a staff of 9 physicians and 400 employees.

1936 Post office located at south end of Hood Building, now E. W. Beck's.

1937 Fire, a disaster on Main Street.

1941 Springfield cares for 3,000 patients.

1941 Sykesville School System serves 588 students.

1941 Fire Department has fire apparatus, but water supply is limited to private wells and river.

1957 High School severely damaged by fire.

1963 Public schools fully integrated.

1968 Public water, sewage and fire hydrants installed.

1968 McDonald House acquired for Town Hall.

1968 Route 32 by-pass opens.

1969 The town annexes 26 acres for Sykesville Apartments.

1980 Fairhaven, a life-care retirement community, opens just outside City limits.

1985 Sykesville Historic District entered on The National Register of Historic Places.

1985 Storm Drain System phase one installed; phase two completed in 1989.

1990 Town acquires railroad station, leases it as restaurant, Baldwin's Restaurant & Pub.

1991 Historic District Commission created.

1997 Town acquires and begins renovation of Sykesville Schoolhouse, 1904-38.

1997 Sykesville Development Corporation created .

1997 Sykesville Gate House Museum of History opens.

1998 Master Plan for Main Street adopted by Town.

1999 Town acquires operating 1948 Model G-12 Train with 4 cars; B&P Railroad, 1911 Interlocking Tower Building planned.

1999 Warfield Complex annexed, adding 138 acres to the town.

INDEX

Italicized numbers refers to photographs.

SYKESVILLE FEDERAL SAVINGS ASSOCIATION

1321 Liberty Road, Eldersburg, Maryland

(Across from Wal-Mart)

410-795-1900, 410-795-4300

Federal Savings Association, located at 1321 Liberty Road, Eldersburg, is a relatively small and conservative bank. With its newly opened facility, it will continue to offer the friendly, personal banking services that it has provided Carroll and Howard County residents since it opened its doors on February 21, 1880.

The Sykesville Perpetual Building Association was organized by dry good merchants Zimmerman and Schultz to assist farmers from the surrounding county in borrowing money. The Association's first meeting was in their store in the spring of 1870. The Association was chartered in 1887 and rechartered and reorganized in 1907 when it became the Sykesville Building Association of Carroll County.

When organized in 1870, loans were auctioned off and sold at a premium as high as 20%. By this process many farmers were assisted in purchasing real estate and building their own homes. In 1908 the Association paid shareholders an annual dividend of 6.5%.

The business was run out of the director's homes until 1922. As the Association grew, office space was rented from local businesses in Sykesville. In 1972 land was purchased on Liberty Road in Eldersburg (Md. Rt. 26), Maryland, where a branch was opened in late September. The MISSIC crisis hit in May of 1985, upon which time the Association applied to the Federal government for our deposit insurance. In September 1985 a building was built to consolidate the two locations into one building. In October 1985 the Association was chartered with the Federal Government. On September 12,1988 the business name changed from the Sykesville Building Association of Carroll County to Sykesville Federal Savings Association.

The summer of 1998 a new structure was erected behind the old building. Moving date was December 14, 1998 into its new facility.

The association has remained profitable throughout its history. Sykesville Federal Savings Association is now a full service bank with assets in excess of 40 million dollars.

Deposits are Federally Insured to $100,000 by Savings Association Insurance Fund. (SAIF).

For local residents who want personal service banking, Sykesville Federal offers a friendly, helpful atmosphere and individual attention that is not found in most larger banks. It has no stockholders; rather, its depositors are the owners, and, therefore, participate in its competitive interest and dividend payments. *Sykesville Federal guarantees continued commitment to service all your banking needs.*

*Success is Built on **Reputation**..*
__Ours Has Been__ Consistently
Growing for 115 Years.

Eldersburg's Only Full Service Locally Owned Bank

DEMCO